Listen Up!

Listen Up!

spoken word poetry

edited by
zoë anglesey

ONE WORLD
THE BALLANTINE PUBLISHING GROUP • NEW YORK

A One World Book
Published by The Ballantine Publishing Group

Compilation copyright © 1999 by Zoë Anglesey
Foreword copyright © 1999 by Yusef Komunyakaa
Afterword copyright © 1999 by Édouard Glissant

Permission acknowledgments can be found on page 198, which constitutes
an extension of this copyright page.

www.ballantinebooks.com/one/

Library of Congress Cataloging-in-Publication Data

Listen up! : spoken word poetry / edited by Zoë Anglesey. — 1st ed.
p.   cm.
ISBN: 0-345-42897-8 (alk.paper)
1. American poetry—20th century. 2. Performance art—United
States. 3. Hip-hop—Poetry. 4. Sound poetry. I. Anglesey, Zoë.
PS615.L47   1999
811'.5408—DC21   98-52065

Cover photos by Robert Hughie
Cover design by Kristine V. Mills-Noble
Book design by H. Roberts Design

Manufactured in the United States of America

First Edition: April 1999
10 9 8 7

This collection of poems is dedicated to
the named and unnamed mentors
who have given the gifts of inspiration and discipline
to these writers
as well as to the makers of this collection.

May we also acknowledge our dear communities
that, with respect and encouragement, embrace
the aspirations of our future writers
as they generously become more committed
to their tasks at hand.

contents

foreword

necromancy

The voices in *Listen Up!* are personal and public, and they also speak on behalf of others. They share a similarity of aesthetics and concerns, but these poems are not spoken from a privileged position; their agency did not spring from an assumption of freedom based on birthright. These young voices have witnessed the voicelessness of loved ones (family and/or community). The poems have not been honed into overconscious literary designs or literature with a capital L. In fact, some moments in *Listen Up!* seem like eruptions, primal cries, outbursts, and jagged incantations (less tonally and structurally conspicuous than Dada and the Black Arts Movement).

Listen Up! could only have been written by a group of young poets such as these in the 1990s. Likewise, the anthology's editor, Zoë Anglesey, is a risk-taker who happens to be a visionary. It seems that some of these voices were directly transfused from the Black Arts Movement twenty years after Isaac Hayes and Pet Rocks. The aesthetics are similar, almost down to the uncapitalized personal pronoun *i*. But the ideological conceits and transparent rage are less on the surface of this poetry of the 1990s. The fighting dreams of the Civil Rights Movement are just below the surface of these voices that are educated and middle-class. And, in this sense, they are more complicated. In fact, the rage in these voices is a by-product of the backlash against the Civil Rights Movement that ushered in the Reagan era. Though there are references to Malcolm X, these poems are not fueled by the back-blast of international moral outrage that surfaced during the sixties and influenced the tone and timbre of the Black Arts Movement. These young voices are not driven by a collective agenda, nor are they shadows of some minor phoenix risen from prophetic ashes. At first glance, however, it seems a safe bet to say that they grew out of rap and hip-hop, poetry slams, the industry of colorful tags, Jean-Michel Basquiat, etc.

There is a trickster motif in *Listen Up!* Each poem negotiates at least two territories simultaneously. Like hip-hop, these voices want to *appear* untutored and, at times, they seem to exist at the nucleus of a class war with themselves. The language of this poetry is textured by popular-culture references and multiple levels of diction—erudite and street-smart. The voices seem fully initiated: hip-hoppers dressed in the baggy regalia of Southern sheriffs of yesteryear and Rasta dreadlocks—decked out in disguises. But the reader or listener is obligated to think about what lingers at the center of each poem. In an era when it could be "unhealthy" or "uncool" to appear as nerdy—the maker of poems—perhaps the poem's attempted disguise is armor for the poet who speaks about things of the heart. Thus, the architecture or appearance fortifies and underlines the trickster-poet's mask.

But the aesthetics of "styling" can be doubly deceptive. In this sense, some of the poems are more akin to the blues tradition than to hip-hop. They seem to be saying, *What you see is what you get.* Although these voices have been filtered through a complex literary tradition (European-African-Asian-Latin-American), the surface of the poetry appears colloquial. *Listen Up!* is mainly a poetry of statements and pronouncements, seldom venturing into that surreal territory many of the Negritude poets embraced through imagery. And there are even a few moments straight out of the R & B tradition of crooning and swooning on the edge of heartbreak—poems aimed at the seduction of mind and body. But thankfully there are more symbolic references and allusions to (re)quest than conquest in this body of highly provocative work.

Consequently, *Listen Up!* begs for performance. Many of the poems lie on the page with ease, but others can only come alive through the human voice: orality pulsates at the center of this anthology. There is limited space in these poems for contemplation and meditation. This is an urban anthology, with a driven trajectory and urgency whereby many of the poems have been shaped into a vertical velocity—for the most part, each poem descends the page swiftly. The short lines are gutsy; they have muscle. At times they are raw and basic as the disquieting lyricism and needful bravado of Ma Rainey and Big Bill Broonzy.

This is a poetry of engagement and discourse—it celebrates and confronts. Its passion cannot be denied or undermined. It might obliterate one reader's *taste*, and facilitate another's. The puns might hit the mark or miss the target, but one cannot claim that these poems have been falsified to exact a fiction or illusion or Edwardian elegance.

Listen Up! arrives on the eve of the twenty-first century, and the jaunty drive and energy in each poem seem to say *Made in America.* This anthology is straightforward. Even with the title's exclamation mark, this is not a scream pouring out of a bullhorn or a cornucopia of evasions through experimentation. These young voices care about human life, and they seem to suggest that anything else is a sham.

—Yusef Komunyakaa
December 1998

introduction

Whenever five-time Apollo-winner Jessica Care Moore entered the Brooklyn Moon Café in the mid-nineties, it was as if the waters parted. Call it charisma, say she had a vibe, but it was Jessica's natural intensity that had the audiences assembled for the Friday night open-mic readings energetically swirling in her wake. Often the young people assembled were so jammed up against each other in this tiny spoken-word digs only four subway stops away from Manhattan that many had to pitch themselves on tiptoe to see Moore in action. Infectious in her enthusiasm, on fire in her delivery, Jessica Care Moore epitomized the spoken word poet. She respected her listeners enough to make every line of her poems pop, and in return some two hundred hands, raised in the air, snapped their fingers in approval.

Even before he starred in *Slam*, the Sundance and Cannes film festivals' award-winning feature, Saul Stacey Williams commanded inordinate attention from his peers. A striking presence, his oratorical style was reminiscent of Paul Robeson. When Williams first appeared before the Brooklyn Moon Café crowds, he was in graduate school at New York University finishing an M.F.A. in drama, with nearly a decade dedicated to his studies in acting. Naturally, this training influenced the way he delivered his poems. Stanza after stanza of his twenty-minute poems cascaded from the scrolls in his head. People seated before him bobbed their heads in time to his musical cadences, as Williams flailed his limber arms much like a conductor or a preacher. His gestures transmitted the nuances of each passage. Saul Williams's readings were unequivocally memorable and remain so.

In the nineties, Moore and Williams, along with Suheir Hammad, Mariahadessa Tallie, Tish Benson, Carl Hancock Rux, Tracie Morris, Willie Perdomo, and Ava Chin, earned considerable distinction at both the Brooklyn Moon Café and the Nuyorican Poets Café in Manhattan. From these venues, they launched careers that now have them traveling the spoken word circuit nationally and internationally. *Listen Up! Spoken Word Poetry* presents these nine scribes and introduces their work to an even wider public.

Youthful and, as they would admit, quite unbeholden to literary formalism, they count themselves among the emerging literati of their generation. The poems collected in *Listen Up!* mainly record their New York experiences. This is not the case, however, with Carl Hancock Rux, who at an early age retraced the footsteps of his mentors from the Harlem Renaissance who had found sanctuary in Paris. Quickly realizing that he could not relive their past, he promptly headed off to explore other parts of the world. His poetry reflects his travels and self-discovery.

Regardless of their birthplaces, journeys, or individual literary and cultural influences, these spoken word poets agree that they have much in common. First, they tested the soundness of their nascent writings primarily in the two cafés that were landmark venues for spoken word. In these demanding settings, they developed their unique styles. The *Listen Up!* poets unanimously defy any notion that they represent a fixed, univocal position. They're too young to be set in their ways, and they also take pride in examining the confining orthodoxies of traditional forms. With this in mind, *Listen Up!* readers will enjoy discovering the range of personas that inhabit each exciting poet.

Even after seeing the documentary film *Slam Nation*, or *Slam*, or any of the other recent films showing a version of the current urban poetry scene, it's still difficult to define what spoken word poetry is. It may be helpful to think of this genre as the fulcrum between opposite points. On one end, traditional, mainstream poetry tends to fit nicely on either the page or the stage, often with a great deal of decorum. When read before the public, contemporary poetry needs few props other than an expressive voice. On the opposite end, the performance arts may combine many elements, including voices, dance, music, and visual and media arts, as well as poems or texts that transmute into monologues or fully developed scripts. Hip-hop, or rap, as a predominantly African-American popular and commercial art form, stands between spoken word and the performance arts. Both spoken word and hip-hop derive from the oral tradition, and both forms appeal to overlapping demographics.

A growing number of newspapers list spoken word events apart from the literary reading and the performance arts. Spoken word is associated with youthful wordslingers who involve themselves in aural graffiti, verbal combat, slam squads, and roving posses of like-minded masters at wordplay. Spoken word poetry can also mean the recitation or reading of poetry that rides on didactic rails of the irreverent rants and coming-of-age rituals. Understandably, physical motion, expressive body language, stance, or gesture is an indelible part of spoken word performance. Also, this poetry often keeps a beat; it accentuates rhythms to move a narrative, and strikes syllabic accents to accentuate the music of a piece or an outrageous punch line.

Spoken word artists of African-American origins also know the legacy of silence or minimal movement imposed by the shackles of slavery—the stilling of indigenous idioms, sundown laws, and codes for concealed expression. Spoken word gives this generation the means to create exclamatory, free and freeing free verse.

Like their mentors who improvised in the jazz or spiritual mode, these poets are challenged by freestyling à la hip-hop. Spoken word affirms passionate, even shocking expression. Because of the age of its main practitioners, spoken word often lingers on sensual themes, or righteously offers ethical and just insights for solving the most severe problems plaguing society.

Poetry has always been "hot" or "cool" within popular culture, and within each generation. Certainly a case can be made that spoken word is like a new wine in old bottles, and that it is a contemporary kind of urban poetry.

Spoken word poets, like the early Beats before them, practice their art in a democratic manner. Open-mic nights at spoken word venues typically have sign-up sheets for all who want to read their poems. First come, first served decides the order. The good, the bad, and the ugly convene happily and respectfully. Celebrity works in the cafés, however, just as it does in the larger society. If spoken word stars walk in, some accommodation is made to fit them into the lineup. On open-mic nights, initiates to spoken word learn their poetics, not by studying Contemporary American Poetry, but the hard way—through audience approval, or disapproval.

In addition to perusing contemporary poetry, the ambitions of the nine poets included in *Listen Up!* have them honing in on other interests as well. As spoken word gravitates more and more toward the performance arts, the poets are venturing into multiart and multigenre writing. Carl Hancock Rux has had over thirty plays produced. He also has produced and stars in his *Rux Revue.* Like any band that releases a CD and then tours, Rux fronts a quartet complete with a trio of divas as backup singers. He performs reciting, singing, and chanting many of the poems from his *Pagan Operetta,* and to original music that borrows mainly from soul and rock.

Tish Benson has exhibited deconstructed poems as visual surfaces; she's also written plays and film scripts. Jessica Care Moore's second play, *There Are No Asylums for the Real Crazy Women*, centers on a dialogue between Vivien Haigh-Wood Eliot, the English wife of renowned poet T. S. Eliot, and Jess, a young poet. This play took its fuller shape from a poem in Moore's book *The Words Don't Fit in My Mouth*. She has recorded with Grammy-nominated jazz altoist Antonio Hart and at this writing is planning a studio recording for the hip-hop market. Saul Williams will see the release of a CD coproduced by Rick Rubin, who launched the Beastie Boys, Public Enemy, and LL Cool J. In other words, these are ambitious, multigenre artists who use their prodigious talents in a multitude of ways.

Historically these poets fit squarely within the African-American literary tradition. Langston Hughes (1902–1967) wrote essays, plays, librettos, fiction, and poems. He translated poetry from several languages, and traveled widely as well. Praised and reviled for embracing revolution, Hughes nevertheless remained astute when it came to geopolitical issues. He expressed his own protests against racism in his written works and in public. The founder of African-American theater companies in Harlem and Los Angeles, Hughes was also recorded reciting poetry on LPs. Clearly, the *Listen Up!* poets do not fall far from the tree.

Amiri Baraka has also been a major mentor to the poets of this volume. In fact, he may be one of the original spoken word artists. In the late fifties and early sixties, he and Ted Joans were among the celebrated poets who became known as the Beats. They congregated in Greenwich Village coffeehouses and private lofts to recite their poems, often to the rhythms of congas and bongos. Baraka, known then as LeRoi Jones, published other avant-garde Beat poets such as Allen Ginsberg, Gregory Corso, Diane Di Prima, and Peter Orlovsky in the literary magazine *Yugen*.

However, in the early sixties, Baraka left the realm of the

Beats because of racism and ideological differences. Baraka not only penned historical statements defining African-American music (*Blues People*, 1963) and poetry (*The Dead Lecturer*, 1964), which critiqued the Eurocentric aesthetic while affirming the values of African-American culture, he also extended his poems into monologues and fully developed plays. By 1965, Baraka had founded the Black Arts Repertory Theater and School in Harlem, dedicated to African-American nationalist values. Interestingly, both Baraka and Joans were called jazz poets, not only because of their musical loyalties, but because they were often called on by jazz musicians to sit in during concerts or recordings.

In fact, it was Ted Joans who created the media image of a Beat poet—usually wearing a beret and a black turtleneck. But Joans is quick to shift the focus away from this image. He says: "The Beat Generation wasn't a way of dressing, it was a state of mind, of spirit. If you pick up *How I Became Hettie Jones*, you'll read how she often saw this guy dressed in black. She asked me once why I wear black this and black that, and I said it was out of necessity. It's better than going to a laundry every other day. That's true. That's it. It's not original. They did it in France. When France came out of World War II, the existentialists dressed in dark clothes because they didn't have the money to have clothes cleaned. That's one of the things that upset people about Allen Ginsberg. Allen said yes, I go to a secondhand store and buy a suit. He never bought anything brand new." As far as what the Beats accomplished, Joans succinctly notes: "We brought poetry to the public. We took it out of the *salons de poésie* that followed the traditions in Europe, especially in England where it was an elitist type of thing. Our generation brought poetry out in the open and we recited in coffeehouses and some bars. In New York they tried to prevent that; places had to have a cabaret license for us to read a poem, just like with the musicians—they couldn't play where they didn't have a cabaret license." Because Ted Joans has lived most of his life in Europe, his influence as a mentor has been felt by and large in that part of the world.

Speaking of the connection between spoken word and hip-hop, Amiri Baraka notes: "It's the same continuum; it just depends on where you get on the train." Jessica Care Moore proudly admits to being influenced by hip-hop's thirty-year lineage and acknowledges that it has wielded considerable impact on spoken word poetry. Elaborating on Baraka's view, Moore says: "Hip-hop and poetry stem from the same thing; it's just that the aesthetics are different. Hip-hop requires music." But she adds: "When I do a show, I have no beats, but at the same time, I can go into the studio with the same material and work with a hip-hop producer to create a poetry/hip-hop CD." Moore raises another point when she says, "Nikki Giovanni was influenced by jazz. . . . Amiri Baraka has been influenced by jazz and the blues. It's just that hip-hop is the music of our day, and so, we're influenced by it."

Taking full stock of the impact of spoken word poets, Moore says: "We definitely have breathed life into this art form, like generations haven't in a long time. A lot of it has to do with the influence of hip-hop music. Rakim's lyrics, KRS-ONE's, Blacksides' lyrics show that they twist their poetry a little bit and call it hip-hop and then they put a beat underneath it, and make some money. It's a billion-dollar industry. Maybe we can make a little bit of that. Maybe we will. If not, I think it will help us put a dent in that mainstream audience." S. H. Fernando Jr., who wrote *The New Beats*, would agree with Moore. He writes: "Hip-hop has infiltrated the mainstream because creativity is a commodity. . . . Rap creates not only artists but businessmen." Even if Moore has her own publishing company, no one can make the case that spoken word, published or recorded, has the commercial appeal that rap enjoys.

Most of the *Listen Up!* poets grew up hearing hip-hop; it is the music of their generation. However, Tracie Morris, Jessica Care Moore, Suheir Hammad, and Saul Stacey Williams show the most influence of hip-hop on their writing and delivery of poetry. Williams rhymed when he was in junior high school, and so he believes it was part of his early development as a poet. Nevertheless, he resents being labeled and categorized. When Williams says he opens for hip-hop acts, he does so assuming it is understood that this merely means he is brought in to do his poetry and that he delivers. Williams turns uncompromising if he notices a pop label coming his way. He doesn't want to be boxed in or confined by the simplicities, and complicities, associated with musical or literary media tags. If he's acting, he's an actor; if he is in front of an audience reciting poetry, he is not performing, nor is he entertaining per se. He wants his art to be perceived as poetry, plain and simple. When Williams improvises center front of a live band, he may relent and use the term of his generation—"freestyling." It's clear, though, that he rejects attempts to fold his art into any easy brand-name category. In response to a caption appearing under a photo promoting *Slam*, Williams said, "I'm not a 'Rapper.'"

A major home base for some of the *Listen Up!* poets in the mid-nineties was at the Brooklyn Moon Café in the Fort Greene section of Brooklyn. The café's proprietor, Michael Thompson, admits that he didn't know much about poetry at first, but he thought poets would bring people into the café, which was what he needed when he first opened.

And bring in the people they did. Soon thereafter, paying five-dollar covers, a host of talented young people converged at the café on Friday nights for the open-mic readings. In summer, the air conditioner couldn't keep the temperature down; wintertime, the steamy windows gave testimony to the heat inside. As the temperature rose, so did the level of excitement. Emcees laid down the ground rules: People were to snap their fingers and not clap out of respect for the tenants living above the café. As for stepping up to the mic, the obligatory conventions included: Keep it short and sweet. "Sweet" meant poets had to be sexy.

Jessica Care Moore, Saul Stacey Williams, Suheir Hammad, and Mariahadessa Ekere Tallie fit the bill, but not at the expense of their multithemed poems. Aspiring initiates—mostly from Brooklyn narrators, orators, lyricists, and rappers—followed suit. They lingered over enjambments that brought together sexual and sensual imagery. After all, the hours from ten until two were prime time for the dating game. Most of the young women in braids, twists, locks, and afros dressed stylishly. Mariahadessa Tallie says, "The guys smelled good (from all those oils); they looked good, with teeth and eyes flashing, and they were charming, too." A whole lot of introducing went on during intermission. Dancing was reserved for Saturday nights. On Fridays, drinking soft drinks or coffee, eating muffins, salmon burgers, or desserts (prepared by Thompson, his brother, and cousins), spoken word fans packed in close to listen to the poets who were their peers.

The grapevine eventually brought in "poetry tourists" and spoken word luminaries from afar—New Jersey, Connecticut, Washington, D.C., and Boston. In fact, the founders of Boston's Afrocentrics, a spoken word club, made several trips to the Moon to scout out contacts before they opened. By 1996 representatives from the press were frequently showing up for the Friday open-mic readings or the "Meet the Author" series on Sundays. Reporters were from New York; even Japanese newspapers and video crews from City Arts aired segments from readings more than once on Channel 13, the local New York PBS TV station. Even more attention was paid to Brooklyn's poetry "Renaissance" when Jessica Care Moore's photograph appeared on the front page of the *New York Times.*

But the open mic at the Brooklyn Moon Café served another purpose as well. It provided freedom of speech on safe ground. Community organizers, political candidates, senior mentors who either reminisced or preached in between poems, Park Slope gadabouts, Manhattanites on a mission, women telling it like it is, and gay poets all came together every Friday night. Tallie says, "It was like a family." One of the headliners at the Brooklyn Moon Café, Saul Williams, said: "We were on the same page," referring to the spirit of community and keen state of awareness of the issues of the day.

But the core group of spoken word poets also debated the merits of the message in their poems. Maybe they could not explain the origins of the spiritual charge in their works, but they knew it was something the crowds wanted to hear. Jessica Care Moore was known for her follow-through. She enthusiastically did as she said. Outlining the "politics versus art debate," Moore says: "I think writing is a form of activism. It's the most seductive sort of activism that I've been able to do. I've tried to get involved with as many support organizations as I can." Then, returning to her talent and her task, Moore adds, "But I think I do a lot more work on my writing. I want to do more theater and film. I really enjoy publishing." And off she goes with a list of projects she is working on.

Writing poetry involves thinking in solitude, dreaming of images, meditating on meanings, and writing down what comes to mind. Thinking gets its fuel from reading literature, history, the sciences, philosophy, and reading the works deemed to be essential within the culture. Ted Joans says, "I grew up with my face stuck in a book. There's the key. Miles Davis said, 'Gonna get an education, on Forty-Second Street there's a big university called the New York Public Library. Spend some time .' It's true."

The poets, whose works have been sampled here, report that the reading they did in their youth provided the connective tissue between the past and future. Joans points out that the Beats were educated and had gone to "expensive" colleges, and those who had missed the train got there another way. For example, Gregory Corso used to sit in on classes at Harvard, or whatever he could get in. Reading definitely provided the point of departure for writing, and it was a prerequisite for so many debates and conversations in the coffeehouses.

When Williams states "We were all on the same page," he also means that literally. The poets who congregated at his house after spoken word shows shared their insights about their readings from poetry, fiction, plays, and even the news. In academic circles, this is called work-shopping. Without doubt, these poets discovered that reading was essential if they were going to progress or reach the literary stature they dreamed of.

Miguel Algarín, cofounder of the Nuyorican Poets Café, and as director of this congenial venue for poetry, theater, and music, set the stage for a freewheeling and copious outpouring of poetry. The café has served as a cultural center over the past three decades in "Loisaida"—Manhattan's Lower East Side, which was once home mainly to Jews and Puerto Ricans. Now the gentrified neighborhood has been renamed the East Village, and still it remains a haven to young artists of every sort. Youth fleeing small-town parochialism, moribund cities, or their own nationalities with hopes of surviving via the green card, convene in the cafés and bars. The Nuyorican Poets Café has always been the hangout for budding artists.

For the *Listen Up!* poets, Algarín was there to produce and stage early plays by Carl Hancock Rux and Jessica Care Moore. The Nuyorican Poets Café named Willie Perdomo (1991), Tracie Morris (1992), Tish Benson (1994), and Saul Williams (1996) its Grand Slam Champs. Algarín was also one of the first anthologists of spoken word poets. Along with coeditor and slam master Bob Holman, he included Tracie Morris and Perdomo, Benson and Williams in *Aloud! Voices from the Nuyorican*. The menu at the Nuyorican Poets Café during any one evening may include open-mic poetry, a play, and a live band. This café has been the cultural headquarters for several generations of poets and fans.

Typically, in a welcome speech that flows into an Afrorican

chant, Miguel Algarín's deep and resonant voice seems to have been blessed by accents equally Boricuan, African, and Shakespearean. To be sure, Algarín is a Shakespeare scholar, just as he is of his Boricuan and African cultures from their indigenous roots to the present. Indeed, by way of an altar with candles and flowers—sometimes fresh, oftentimes plastic, depending on the abundance of the coffers—the Santería orishas bless and protect the café and all within. With Algarín's guidance and blessings, several generations of artists have moved on to have books published, plays produced, and movies made.

On behalf of the poets in *Listen Up!* our gratitude goes out to Miguel Algarín, a major force in creating the latest wave of interest in poetry—spoken word. Other prominent mentors to the poets represented here are Amiri Baraka, The Last Poets, and Ntozake Shange. Thanks go out to them for their enduring inspiration. Cheryl Woodruff, Associate Publisher of One World Books, suggested that *Listen Up! Spoken Word Poetry* be published. I thank her for initiating the project, as well as her staff for their support. I also wish to thank my literary agent Susan Ginsburg and her assistants. The work stayed on course with words of encouragement from friends Pia and René López, Lori Leistyna, Chi Chi Hare, and poets Gail Hall and E. Ethelbert Miller. With deep feelings of gratitude, I thank Yusef Komunyakaa and our young poets for their contributions to *Listen Up!* These poets are among the writers I love, sharing as they do, their free-hearted art, which is life itself.

Listen Up!

© TISH BENSON

tish benson

WWhen asked about the first times that she wrote down her thoughts, Tish Benson explains: "Well, I had a diary when I was a little girl . . . stuff like . . . 'I know it's been a whole year since the last time I wrote in this thing but I am going to write in it every day 'cause I need to talk to somebody' . . . then I wouldn't write in it for another six months or a year."

As for her debut reading a poem, Benson, her manner of speaking revealing her Texas roots, spins the story of how an aunt gave her a child's book of verse on her eighth birthday. Enticing the girl and her two brothers to memorize the poems, the aunt put up a prize of five dollars. Her smile showing her pleasure at the memory, Benson recalls: "My younger brother and I, we were like, 'Yes! Okay!' So we did it—'Under the spreading chestnut tree, the village smithie stands,' yeah! That's so crazy . . . it was the first time I got paid for reciting poetry."

Another encounter with the art occurred when Benson was studying for a B.A. in anthropology at the University of Oklahoma. She recalls, "I was going out with a guy, and he was reading this literature book with poetry in it. I looked at it and said, 'Yuk!' He said, 'Yeah? Have you ever really tried reading poems?' I said, 'I hate poetry.'" Her voice rising at the recollection of the challenge, Benson continues. "And so he read a poem. I don't remember what, but I said, 'Oh, wow! That's nice.' He just read it with so much feeling. I was like, 'That was too beautiful.'"

Benson's next major move brought her to the Big Apple. As for her motivation, she says, "It hit me one day that if I stayed here [Houston, Texas] I would forever be mediocre, and though, at the time, I didn't know what I was good at or if I was good at anything, I knew I wasn't mediocre." A year into living in New York, Benson heard about a writers' workshop conducted by Quincy Troupe. Of this experience, she remarks: "We read to each other, critiquing each other's poetry. We were trying to work it out—versus now, when you hear, 'Yo, I got a gig.' We didn't approach it that way."

Benson's vision of how one moves from creating on the page to the arena of open mics in cafés and clubs came into clear focus after she heard Reg E. Gaines reel out poems that he had memorized. "I felt like, 'Wow, I wanna go there,'" says Benson. "That's taking it to the next level to be able to work your words on stage." However, Benson remains adamant about the need for writers to read literature. She's read the canon of African-American plays, much poetry, and she emphasizes that this is essential for "crafting a poem."

Throughout the nineties, Tish Benson often frequented the stage at the Nuyorican Poets Café. On the mic either as a take-no-prisoners poet or an MC, Benson spun her introduction to poems, to poets, to the goings-on, lavished with her gutsy vernacular. If an audience seemed a little too passive, Benson skillfully laid down a few provocative lines that gave the crowd plenty of reason to either do a double-take or double over in laughter. In moderating spoken word proceedings, Benson's humor definitely lightened up matters, especially if someone's poetics failed to connect. Gifted with a knack for repartee, Benson might keep the flow going and slip everybody smack dab in the middle of one of her own poems built upon the blues ritual of call and response.

For all this, Benson was awarded the Nuyorican Grand Slam Championship in 1995. The following year, Benson received an

Artist's Fellowship from the New York Foundation for the Arts for her play *Giant Steps at Smalls Bar*. The NYFA fellowship allowed her, she says, "to buy a computer and hang out at cute coffee shops."

During this time she pondered her future. Benson leveled with herself: "It's rough when ya gotta call home for some money and momma jus' as broke as . . ." Benson figured, "I was born to sing the blues." But she admits, "Now, I really can't sing and that's another problem, but since I was born to sing the blues and I can't, then I write the blues and perform the blues and, unfortunately, I live the blues." Benson reflects for a moment and then says, "Well, maybe it's fortunate, 'cause if I couldn't write the blues and perform them, then what else would I be here for?"

Another side of this poet comes to light when Benson says, "Poetry can be soothing." Poetry is not only public but, for her, it is personal and solitary. Benson creates visual art from her poems that may be placed on exhibit or go to friends as gifts inked on handmade papers. Considering the long-term exigencies of living in this society, Benson has invested in a ticket, she hopes. In the spring of 1999, Benson received a master's degree in the Dramatic Writing Program from New York University. With this credential in hand, she looks forward to finalizing her tenure as "a broke-ass poet crying the blues."

A writer with varied interests, Benson has moved beyond wanting to see her words just on paper or winning slams. Benson hopes to see her words—which often come from voices she can impersonate at the drop of a hat—dramatized by actors on the silver screen. Benson says dryly, "I would like to make a fabulous living off my writing."

For an exhibit titled *No Doubt: African-American Art of the 90's*, a wall of words created by Benson was installed at the Aldrich Museum of Contemporary Art in Ridgefield, Connecticut. In addition, Benson has organized spoken word performances at the American Craft Museum in Manhattan, the Brooklyn Children's Museum, and a multitude of cafés and stages that flourish on Manhattan's Lower East Side. Her writings have been published in *Long Shot* (in a special anthology issue edited by Danny Shot); *In the Tradition: An Anthology of Young Black Writers*, edited by Kevin Powell and Ras Baraka; and *Verses That Hurt: Pleasure and Pain from the Poemfone Poets*, edited by Jordan Trachtenberg. Benson has been recorded on the CD compilations *Flippin the Script: Rap Meets Poetry* and *The Mango Room*. She performs with the jazz/hip-hop band Three Bean Stew.

i got tha boogaloosa fever
dedicated to Yusef Komunyakaa

U Boogaloosa booga

I wanna sit on yo brain
take notes while u conjure up phrases
that don't cotton to fixed realities

while u mold Neon Vernaculars
into monster beats never heard before
I wanna float on yo cerebellum

I wanna be yo eye drops: clear liquid
soothing wild
dark
beautiful places
where images take wings and sing

I wanna be High on Sadness
completely
Lost in the Bonewheel Factory

I wanna walk the red Louisiana clay dirt
absorb its healin properties and transpose metaphors of you to
    paper

I want my tongue to do the Komunyakaa flip
turnin words into platinum while stayin a chill poppa stoppa
(go on with ya bad self) . . . yeahh

I wanna go to the pit of yo soul
afix myself between it and a moon in full bloom

croonin for u like a bayou geechie woman in heat and thankin God
that the world will know what shoulda been all along:

u a bad Boogaloosa Louisiana booga

p.s. next time u in town we'll have a jambalaya fest and if the
crawfish kickin we'll bite off the heads/bite into the tails and wash
it all down with the firewater of yo choice.

Big love atcha Yusef.

processions

There are words that pass for charms
No one knows better how to use them than the ace of spades
Master Chameleon! Llegba's Mentor!
See Watch
As the eye lets in light
Light becomes cloud
Cloud / wind
Wind dances around juke joints
to fill needful things . . .

baby when I asked you to write a poem bout me I was talkin bout one
of them love is splendid thangs poems baby I was talkin bout one of
them yo lips taste like sweet nectar from Gods divine loveliness poems I
was talkin bout one of the inseparable poems . . . you know like Natalie
Cole sang way back in tha day . . . Llegbas mentor? baby thats deep . . .
cold blooded . . . I aint no trickster . . . dont I come see you even if I
gotta jump a turnstile?

You all netted imbedded
In crooks and crannies
No one not even I knew about
Got inside and worked it like I dreamed
you up
Mighty Mojo Conjure Man
Lucifer's Copilot
I did the snake charmers dance at yo command
Became possessed with mmmmm's and ahhhhh's
when we strangled into one another . . .

oh! . . . ok I'm gettin it now . . . imma sucka . . . u been playin me . . .
yeah tha shit gettin real clear now baby I loved you hard and this the

*thanks I get! . . . I took off from work so I could be there when you got
off . . . and I guess you forgot about that time when I brought Rahkela
over to meet u . . . we all went to the park . . . she really liked you
baby . . . and for what! so you could write shit to make folks thank her
daddy put a fix on you? that I did some pimp shit to you? I aint nevah
strangled you gul . . . u mean to me real mean.*

There are thoughts that cloud my eyes
knot up my spine
infiltrate my pores
And I'm not one for such mementos
keeping wrenched remembrances to live in
they serve as tools
Learn from go on
not something to pack around day to day
So I try not to let serenading images go any further
don't need tainted keepsakes
they weigh ya down when it comes to
movin on.

*So this it? . . . u breakin up with me right? . . . man this some cold
hearted shit u doin girl . . . thats how it is . . . some women like kickin
a man when he down . . . yeah dont nobody write about this shit when
a man love hard like me and get tha big boot . . . baby I cant believe u
gone let a hundred dollars come between us . . . why u gotta focus on
negativity? didnt I buy u some earrings that time and what about that
time my boy hook me up with them fish dinners . . . didnt I brang u
some? or what about that time I found that watch and who I give it to?
I coulda sold that watch baby but I gave it to you . . . or what about
alla them times? alla them times alla them good times? you forgot that
didnt ya? yeah but I see it good now . . . u aint never loved me like I
loved you . . . jus cause I aint no poet dont mean I aint got feelins . . .
and there u go steppin on'um with steel plated combat boots . . .
u wrong baby and u treat me bad too.*

he called it a blessin

When undesirable situations manifest themselves
say like ya broke
dog dies
bike stolen
and tha run down draggy feelin
squeezes loud enough
takin hold of insides like no other hardcore vice known
she appeared
Had the lotto win effect
He was cool though
maintained maximum composure while figurin out
zactly
how to get baptized in her waters
Knew it was gone be spiritual regeneration
generatin high energy velocity
A blessin
I mentioned that—right? That—that was what he called it?
Roots churned
cause she was on fire
a hot number he wanted needed
solace something to ease a man's burden
help put the train back on the track now how to give a good
     head rub
Loop de loops n slips n slides
vibrated up his spine
sure sign it was gone be spinnin wheel time
aint tryin to rhyme
it was real
So he made motions to get in her way but to have it appear the other way
round

like she had tried to step in his direction first
Didnt work
Move 2: "Oh excuse me"
His bump in the nite cause that was what he did p.m. time
appeared to be
(him hopin strong)
a misplaced push
by the masses of nite train travelers on to him on to her
She look back rolled eyes
understood more than what he gave her credit for
continued introduction: "So . . . you live around here?"
She nodded quick attemptin to side step his steps as she stepped up her
steps and up the steps to the outside
(not being in the mood for idle conversation)
He continued 3rd time now the charm: "Yeah I just moved around
here . . . seems to be pretty cool . . . names Panther . . . whats u'rs?"

She looked at him like torrential vapors comin down
spewin forth all wrath stored up after 8 hours of her no thanks
     day gig

Disturbed not defeated he ducked icy eyeball volts
boltin towards him
came back with the real charmer
"Oh my mistake . . . 4th time is the shonuff thriller
dealin with sistahs of the Brooklyn brown persuasion"
They don't play that jive hubba hubba
lessin it's coated with honey or pepper sauce
He carried a quart of each plus herbal libations

here it was
Drum roll please: "Hey don't get mad imma nice guy"
Ultra Brite smile

Barry White baritone gone mellower
obsidian drenched skin
shaved head
yeah '90s look oh lawdy pass the bread to sop with please
plus he was doin that mannish reek
(funny how she hadn't notice him in all his splendor before . . .
      musta been
oh never mind thats another bald headed story)
back to: The Mannish Reek
You know what I'm talkin bout that hint of smell good cologne
mixed with summer sweat
lips of life and eyes to bathe by
not no short bath either but one of them
l   o   n   g
d   r   a   w   n   o u t
bubbles galore
scented candles
little satin pillow to prop ya head up with
some Baduizm commin through the speakers . . .
Yeah he was reekin sweet after the hook sunk in her
so yappity yap Ha-ha ha ha's
She upped the 7 digits
no make that 21
voice mail
work and Home
it was gettin good to her then
all that en guard shit
like she was preparin for a fencin duel
went out tha door
Called.   Met him at his day gig.   Exchanged first gifts.
All by day 3
(part of the rope a dope charm ya know . . . panther moves)
Things happen quick when you travelin on vibe time

So
fast forward to . . .
Warrior boogalooing
Brunchin over '70s circa Ebonys
poppin offa walls . . .
Did I tell ya tha brother could sang too?
Mattress alleyooping
reachin sea level   interplanetary travelin
pink hearts yellow moons green clovers
'n stars 'n stars as far as the eyes can see . . .

Then he
backed off
Panther moves
hard times had eased up see
started turnin into good times . . . (no not that J.J. shit)

The Blessin
had worked
Good Grip
powerful backfield in motion
with some awesome biscuits and gravy . . . sistah could cook
washed away Whys? Whats goin ons?
Plaguin him before they met
things was lookin up
gettin bright
light blue skies
and then another's eyes
He preferred "exotique" like kumquats
gingko
le fleur
masala

Said all was not figured with past configurations
"Need to clear some other stuff up . . . lets just be friends"
Said "I aint gonna forget how you made me feel like ten men . . . know what
i'm sayin . . . u got tha good shit girl . . . we gone stay in touch"
She smile clear
decided not to interject with injections of wailin blues
her hue had been spewin since
the Middle Passage
Decided not to break out the butcher knife
slashin jabbin cryin: "Mix this! mutha fucka! and this! 'n this!"
Instead: "Yeah its been fun glad u on your feet again baby"
See she had been there before
fillin spaces buildin mountains
allowin them/him to be
Strengthened
off her nectar
So it wasn't no bitter sadness in her gleam
everybody's gotta have a callin
a mission
a reason for being
Givin out *ital* food so ez
put her in the pantheon of supremeness
(I aint talkin Motown neither . . . well maybe Flo)
But more like Yemenya
Oshun
Billie
Bessie
spirits whose lace cover her shoulders
and who too have been known to give out blessins.

no parts spared

excerpt (for Sabaah)

woke up today
surprised myself
stray bullets poppin inside me like radiated icicles
dreamin this was
The Day
body would finally
loosen up enough
so real me
could go on about my business
flesh and bones holdin on
with a python's clutch
like I aint got stuff to do
without being weighed down
in this 100 pound cemented suit
lead bound feet
hands dipped in acid rain
now this aint no travelin boat I'm in
a war hit ship
hazard waste infested
pesticide injected,
my spirit struggles against a spiked iron lung
belly full of molten crabs
and a pack of rabid dogs scratching my throat
so it's nearin

untitled I

A blood spillers paradise

this place has made a mockery of spiritual revolution

souls into gravel pits

a heart's identity is no longer revealed thru eyes
or words
or deeds

Vampires carry crosses now

cowry shells saronged around hips

wear jazz like an honor badge

paint murals of daytime play

Bright light whoremonger feeding off thoughts
ur spirit dances to their words

surrender pull down guarded walls
release the core of your being

Ur essence flows up their nostrils
till feeding time is done

they belch
laugh   move on

NOTE. Look for parts of you stuck between back teeth
they seldom floss there.

Blue phlegm coats this place
                              truths are tainted
two faced nature boys masked in tropical candyman suits
pockets filled with fantastical mirages
sell u half built bridges
encourage power walks

PLEASE BE WARNED!!!

untitled II

i
spent out
heat of exhaustion
him being more so than me
or so it seemed
puffin triple beats
5th power riffs
head rotatin on its own axis
body flinchin
phantom slaps
syncopated hips squirmin
sheet
twisted in sweat
rope style
between thighs / fingers
like a homemade bungee cord
mouth half opened
eyes half closed
left foot slung over bare mattress
Oscar winnin performance: Best Portrait of a Hungover Limb
other foot sunk deep into deflated pillow
he was laid out.
        that'll keep um

Zake's *get-it and feel-good* script flipped
givin off nuthin but
steam and a toe twitch
Saturn's tiara tilted
sprinklin glitter cross the galaxy
nite clouds genuflected at moon's altar

I knew a nice nod would soon be my touchstone groove too
we pressed chest against chest
spasms ripplin
shrivlin to oblivion.

OK now feedin time is done I aint gone be late for work tomorrow
like I have been for the past month
cause yo ass wanta play farmer all nite long.
Sleep real well baby—I love you.
               a silent affirmation said 3 times quick
tongue flicked his left shoulder
rolled into sleeping spoons position
eyes shut
air pulled in . . . released
pulled in . . . released
slow-tight
like a give n go tug a war match
breath as rope
rope as memory
stretchin back
                passages dug to past landscapes
burnin sands already crossed
stretchin back
seeds blown
stretchin stretchin.

ii

first time hangin out
conductor's car our love mobile
twoness as oneness wrapped around each other
scrunched pact in the corner pocket
we take lookers
on the scenic route

yeah sweetness lemme lay my cheek on ya shoulder
scratch ya itch with this head full of tree parts
way gone new uprisings
a recyclable wannabe rolls cross the floor
atomic skies squeezin out dark
slow
stingy
like it wanna savor nite mysteries from the inside
we copy
playin stirred up rumblins low down
give a nose nudge
         chin pinch
             giggle at each other's funny faces
but this is the sage train:
             ancient shamans
             middle passage ship jumpers
             sojourners marchers
they know

lean into themselves
eye dap
sombody's momma gives a mardi gras grin in our direction
better days may have seen her better but her best days was yet to come
Yall hold on to that . . . not enough of it going around . . .

iii
I saw you first he says to me
I saw u before that
yeah?
Yeah.
A xylophone stitched cross your neck
u pinched skin pullin jazz from caves vampires fear to tread
(streets blunted on yo dowop begged sanctified callins)

rib cage shackled in b-notes
organ grinds and holy water
wiziddry drippin from your finger tips
no shirt
no shoes
tangoin down this rose petal beach
the composer scratchin his phatest symphony
chords ringin waves and tides
only u havin the power to hear
"Oh I see . . . so . . . who spoke first?"
well we communicated telepathically
"but of course"
well, yeah . . . no need to allow our lust messages to . . .
"Lust messages? So that's what it was?"
Well yeah for the most part   that's how it starts . . . really
"ok then what?"
Well that's it . . . we were succinct . . .
your groove was my groove we just knew
"so we got our groove on . . . is that right?"
Yep. Telepathic groovin . . . it was beautiful. u don't remember?
"Yeah that but that was when time was as is
I'm talkin bout before . . . i'm talkin bout the first time around
when it was: feel the notes . . . the melody will follow
                   feels notes close in on fa real beats . . ."
                            drift to clearer consciousness . . .

when we were notes . . .
Just covered in skin . . .

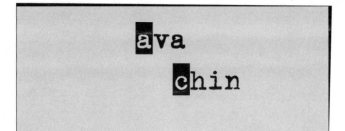

ava chin

born in Flushing, Queens, Ava Chin memorized a good part of Samuel Taylor Coleridge's "Kubla Khan" at age ten and started keeping numerous journals. Chin explains, "Writing was a good way to control the chaotic world of elementary school." Chin, whose grandmother taught her to type, produced her first novel all in capital letters. "It was a murder mystery," Chin says, "in which the evil twin did it—a contrived story line, but not a bad attempt for a sixth grader."

From the start, Chin seems to have had a writing career in mind. She was on the staff of her junior high school yearbook, a contributor to the literary section, and in the late eighties, she was the editor in chief of her high school paper. At Queens College, where she majored in English, Chin recalls, "I sat in on a graduate class where I was exposed to playwrights like Ntozake Shange, Adrienne Kennedy, Caryl Churchill, LeRoi Jones [Amiri Baraka], and Karen Finley. It really opened my eyes." Finishing college with honors and several writing awards, she considered becoming a professional writer, but experienced moments of self-doubt. She says, "I asked myself, how are you going to make a living off that?"

A year after graduating, Chin started freelancing for *The Village Voice* and *Time Out New York*, honing her journalism skills by covering music, film, and underground poetry events. She has written about sex shops in Times Square, martial arts schools in

Chinatown, and poetry events on Manhattan's Lower East Side and in Brooklyn. Critiquing the downside of her profession, Chin states: "In journalism, everything is reduced to a copy quota. Sometimes I prefer the freer expressions of fiction and poetry." She has been on staff at *SPIN* and *VIBE* magazines, and has contributed stories to *Paper* and *A. Magazine*.

While writing for magazines on day gigs, Chin has also explored her creative side by performing on the spoken word circuit in various clubs, theaters, and cafés. As a spoken word performer, she has been on stages in Prague, Berlin, and Hamburg. *Taz*, a German newspaper, wrote that Chin's poetry reflected "the heat and noise of the metropolis." Chin has presented work at the Knitting Factory and the Nuyorican Poets Café, in addition to collaborating with choreographers at the Dance Theatre Workshop and Dixon Place. Chin's only regret while reading at Woodstock '94 was that she didn't "jump into the mud with the crowd when the big rains blew in."

Chin's prose is included in *Sex, Drugs, Rock 'n' Roll: Stories to End the Century*, edited by Sarah LeFanu, and *Dick for a Day: What Would You Do if You Had One?* edited by Fiona Giles. Her poetry appears in *Not a War: American Vietnamese Fiction, Poetry, and Essays* and the literary journals *A Gathering of the Tribes* and *Excurses*. Recently, she cowrote lyrics with the alternative rock band Soul Coughing, even though she says, "I can barely sing." Chin is a 1997–1998 fellow in fiction at New York's Asian-American Writers Workshop.

writers and lawyers

"All the successful writers are lawyers,"
she says, turning full in her chair.
We nod, we murmur, pouring wine
into glasses, watching our reflections
their gypsy dances as the waiter
clears the table. She fingers a hole larger
than a quarter in her sweater.
Like all good English majors of past and
present we have thought the same.
No more shoe-box kitchens and miniature
lives, peering through comfort like a gated
wall to Gramercy Park. Our parents were the
last to enter the gilded hall, but left the key dangling
a foot from the door, ten paces out of reach.
(It is difficult to concentrate when rent is due.)
"Maybe I should apply to law school,"
she sighs as the candle flickers out
and the check appears like a death wish.
But we are gracious, tipping the waiter
desiring the offer to pay, realizing our purses
too thin. We kiss, we part, fingers wide,
faculties open, folding our papers
our precious books like lost dreams and intangible mantras
sluicing the last of the coffee across our teeth
counting the streetlights to the station
praying to the subway gods at 2nd Avenue.
Angry when they do not come.

jetty

Boogie boarders and surf boys
A man floats in the water
He checks the sky and then his watch
The cell phone rings on the shore
A call that goes unanswered.
Toddlers in beach diapers, stumbling as they walk
Carelessly skirt the ocean's edge.
"That's how you have to be," says my sister
skin deepening in the August light
"Fearless like a boy."
The mothers watch from blankets
thrown crisscross stitch work
swollen ankles passed through bathing trunks
arms flung into sweatshirts.
Yelling if they wander too far.
"Jetty! Jetty!" (sunk in the water
strong enough to split a young foot
open before it is full grown)
but the boys will be men who never listen
rushing into the rapid tide.
The women will shout as loud as a whisper
warnings too sudden
too late, too critical
into the turning wave.
A wall of water.

perfect diction

In my dreams while I weep
The television blinks on and off
You unravel my words like so many strands
of my blond hair which falls to the floor
I couldn't make you stay.

I, too, grew to love them so unlike you
raven hair like the flight of
Chinese mission miners in Wyoming
of Filipinos tilling the California land.

When I dream and when I sleep
My Clairol hair cascades in White Cloud curtains.
And I will love whom I love despite
the color of their skin
And you will love whom you love despite
the Guilt.

Looking past the tribal beat
along the archipelago trail
face towards the sun
The Monkey Kings and Queens
travel West
to court pink house towns
and alphabet cities
to follow salsa and jazz
Seattle scenes and gothic strings.
Your face shrank small from my view.
As we danced along the sun-bleached shores
of Angel Island and Brighton Beach

I changed partners
living hand to hand, mouth to mouth
You, too, learned to love without me
And we walked the pavement in
courtly gestures our
jade bangles and quilled feathers
cast aside.

It was difficult to find you
though you were the only Asian in the crowd
And others ate parts of you
a delicate hors d'oeuvre.

I wanted to tell you while I dreamed
and while I wept
I understood when you said
"She was that perfect combination
Asian American
Beautiful yet Distant
Exotic without an Accent."
For in a land where we are not the universe center
We accept *only* the most Beautiful
the most Proper
Prizing our
most perfect
Diction.

winter

When we learned the language our grandmothers
spoke
it was to weave fabric from past to future
Not economics to compete in the job market
Not practicality 'cause that's what everyone
would be speaking.
We learned the antiquated
language of dialects gone awry
Kitchen table talk
Chatter in a box
Language of white haired ladies'
wizened fingertips
Peasant talk
Restaurant clutter made clean by
swilling tea grinds on the table.
On the table
        On the table you put your feelings
        in a box and said they were whole
        Wholly mine a moth-eaten sweater
        buried under layers of clothing
        even in the strongest winter I'll never wear.
        Wear it on your heart
        on your sleeve
        in your smile
        on your face.
        I kiss you with my
        grandmothers' language
        and still you speak to me a slow smile
        A warm breeze before it lifts the hills
        and is gone.

On the picket line we circle breath
we make track marks in the snow
And I learn more and more of her language
and protest.
Booi Got is boycott
Gee Chi is support
My Chinese is a hot pot of Marxist ideology
worker rhythms and rants
peppered with practicalities like, "Where is the bathroom?"
Mistaking the intonation for "Take this" for this "whiteness"
confusing "chicken" and "eat" for "explanation."
Explanation.
You gave me more excuses than I asked for so
I shut the door on explanations.
The snow piled up in the hallway.
In the winter of '35 he told her
on the corner of Bayard and Mulberry
I've gone to China and back and find
you're too American for me.
(Later, he designed the layout for Confucius Plaza
one of the most bourgeois structures for middle income
dollars in Chinatown.)
"That piece of modern-day filth,"
she said, "is what you call 'Chinese'?"
If I could breathe her in and out of me
would I be able to sew the most intricate garment
with the lightest thread?
And these phrases now stumble on smooth as scuffed
silk binding winter summer fall
intergenerationally
will they save our stories from the folds of history
traveling this way and back
halfway around the world?

The world   When I asked for the world you gave me a marble
small and hard
jiggling in my pocket
Ready to be flung to Beijing and back
Capable of rolling across the floor
On the floor you pinned me
Like a spider on a lens
Each word was reason for another bruise
So I packed up my mouth with old cloth and newspaper
and promised to swallow them whole.
    Hole
I buried her bones in a hole
while my boots turned the snow into sludge
through I churned the earth repeatedly
and spoke the words to revive her
that day even her language only spoke to me of snow.
Snow like your heart
In the corners of your smile
You kissed me in Beijing
I lost you in New York
like my language
like her Kindness
gestures of
Revolution and love.

piano concerto

On the second floor of the Hotel Wales
a piano player's fingers produce early New York jazz
while elderly women murmur approval in French
clapping loudly in foreign dialect from upholstered chairs.
They listen for sounds of the city through strains of
Gershwin choreography echoing elevated platforms
and the beat of a young metropolis.
Outside on Madison Avenue, a bus travels north to East Harlem
pushing recirculated air, the fluorescent lights flickering
A grey-haired woman with bloated bags
makes her way sullenly down the aisle.
She knows the sound of New York
it is in her bones when she bends to take a seat.

Up the darkened street a fire engine rushes past
the bodega, startling the Mexican fruit arranger
its sirens pounding red against the tired asphalt.
Still the piano player mixes Stravinsky with Gershwin
the cool evening of her fingers extinguishing flames
that only you inspired, and I, who hurried to put them out.
If I told you I loved you, it would be an unnecessary weight
A pull I no longer have interest in consummating.

The piano player sits unrepentant in black
shifting in spike heels, satin pants
sliding monochromatically against the belly of
gold gilt, the shimmer of money.
Backstage, her dressing room is lined with
ammonium bouquets and hand towels,
the Hotel logo soiled in front.

"Someone to Watch Over Me"—the familiar encore
while the ladies nod appreciatively, the mirror of their teeth
gleaming in time to the syncopated rhythms
of the piano player's finale smile.

Who knew Gershwin could be so sentimental that night
in 1924, tapping into frenetic pulse of rapturous, productive age?
"An experiment in Modern Music," is how I heard you
smelled your footsteps, sitting in the half-light
discerning the pattern of your call. Thump.
The phone that does not ring.
And neither you, nor the ladies, nor the woman on the bus traveling
through Harlem and the Heights, nor Stravinsky, Rachmaninoff, or
Gershwin himself, will ever be able to prove otherwise.

toi san

We lie in the tombs of our beds
A Greek chorus
Forecasting rain and shadow and doom
Listening to water through the hole in the drainpipe
As my uncle brushes his teeth.
This is Toi San on a cloudy day
Where my grandfather kicked his books at the tutor
Years before the gestation of Communism
And he left the mountains to sail to the West
To become a waiter.

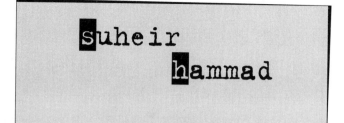

Suheir Hammad

Suheir Hammad was born in a refugee camp in Amman, Jordan, to Palestinian parents. She recalls her first experience with poetry: "I was in the sixth grade, my aunt at the time was head of the English department of Jordan University, and she gave me a young adult version of Edgar Allan Poe's biography. It was filled with drama, alcoholism, and sex. So after reading about his life, I read his poetry." These poems inspired her to graduate from children's books to reading Shakespeare, Tolstoy, Chekhov, and literary short stories. Poetry in its oral form was always part of her life. Hammad fondly says: "My father sang Palestinian songs, many of them based on poems by young soldiers or mothers. I was also aware that God sent down poetry for us to live by."

Unable to endure the bombing of Beirut and the devastation from the ensuing civil war, the Hammad family fled the refugee camps to settle in the Sunset Park area of Brooklyn, New York. With scenes of warfare indelibly fixed in her young mind, Suheir Hammad began another phase of her schooling. Moving among the diverse African-American, Puerto Rican, and other immigrant communities recent and old, Hammad joined her peers in identifying with the hiphop generation. But not everyone in her neighborhood went to school, or admired the new cultural heroes. Crack cocaine and other social ills loomed just beyond the door of the Hammad household. Despite those circumstances, Hammad excelled as a student. She treasured her goals and aspirations, for they were her family's as well.

Soon after Hammad entered Hunter College, she fell under the spell of poets Audre Lorde, June Jordan, and Nawal El Saadawi. Hammad muses: "The first time I heard people reading their poetry was in college; it was incredible. June Jordan had a book titled *Things That I Do in the Dark*. I didn't know before then that I could write down my secret dreams."

At nineteen, Hammad borrowed a word processor. She began to transcribe memories, impressions, and experiences—everything that preoccupied her—and also the rhythmic patterns of her speech. A natural cadence dictated the line breaks. There she had it: poetry. Shortly afterward, her first poems were published, and for this work she received the 1995 Audre Lorde Poetry Award from Hunter College.

Eventually her writing, delivered in performance on the spoken word scene during the early nineties, resulted in a book of poems, *Born Palestinian, Born Black*. Observations of alcoholism, sexism, racism, and political oppression serve as the fulcrum over which her most sensual poems remind the readers, or listeners, that hers is the voice of a young woman deeply in love with life. Hammad's memoir, *Drops of This Story*, traces her survival in war zones as a Palestinian and the drug and gang zones of Brooklyn as an adolescent girl. Reflective of Hammad's output are a forthcoming illustrated children's book; two poetry collections, *Pariah* and *Zaatar Diva*; and an autobiographical film shot in New York and Palestine entitled *Half a Lifetime*.

The music of Hammad's poems, while tinged by hip-hop rhythms, takes flight in response to her ardent desires. She believes a poem's range should embrace community, and to this end, she sets out to create "movement" in the fullest sense of the word. This, then, becomes her own criterion for what makes engaging poetry. She says, "When I'm really moved by a poem, I say 'Yo! I can almost hear the bones breaking in this poem.'"

angels get no maps

i

just some wings   heart
and a destiny to find
you mine

i adapted to your
breath while i slept
did you know
i saw heaven in your
smile heard gospel
in your laugh
you my number
seven   my east

my hip
the hop
finished each other's
thoughts called each other
at the same time
the right time
our conversation rhymed

i'm trying to write
this as though we ain't
over as though you
comin back
but you never
got a map

busy spreadin
wings let go
my hand

and i have yet to learn how
to say goodbye
to those
i love
so i
write them poems too late
and everyone leaves all over
again
this is for you
angel

ii
you carry the *kaabah* in your
head the symbol the stone of
the original covenant
between god and man and me
like a good muslim
i circle you seven times
counter clockwise startin
at your right foot and up

you carry *zam zam*
in your belly and like
my mother hagar i
run between
safa and *marwah*
bed stuy and bushwick
lookin for water

sucklin my young
at your well

you came from the island
of *sarandils* the hills
of eden was your forbidden
fruit weed or malt
do you remember the salt
of the earth your birth

are you the first son
the only son
the last son
the lost son
the sun to my moon
the son who leaves

the son who forgets
you got no map
and this world don't
offer a clue won't
help you
get back
to goodbye to good to god
where you come from

and like a good woman
i make hajj to your door
a skin for the secrets
of the cosmos lookin
for myself in the black
cloth of your hands
the *medina* of your face

iii

and me angel
i'm tryin to write this
in honor of your divinity
but i keep thinkin
bout how lonely
it is to write bout
someone instead of
bein with someone

and i miss your holiness
and all that
but i miss the man
you are and the
man i love

if my love were
enough it would
mend your flight
lighten your load
and remind you
god

seven times i've run
between you and my heart
tryin to help navigate you
love you
enough
alone i write this
for you
and fold my wings

over my heart
fear from hurt
my belly burnin desert

hopin our destiny
is eternity
is shared
is yet
to come

daddy's song

you always loved classics / said
new music was shit / just
like comedians couldn't make jokes / without
getting nasty no more
singers couldn't sing

in your day there was sinatra presley
(you hated him / wouldn't let us watch his flicks)
and some cat named
sam cooke

all the time / "sam cooke can sing sam
cooke sang real songs
simple and real"

i was in high school / the first
time i heard your mix tape of
cooke classics and / i fell
in love with his voice / smooth / smooth

and i fell in love with
the daddy i thought / all
this time talking about
some sinatra presley like guy
not this sweet / sweet music

i was in college when we rented
malcolm's life on video / and the one
good thing spike lee ever / did was

play that song / your song
as denzel / i mean malcolm / was getting
ready to die

you cried in your easy / boy reclining
your head to better listen / it was you
born by the river
daddy / in a little tent
and i swear you been running
running ever since

that's my song too daddy
and one day i'm gonna sing it
for you / in a poem

nother man dead

where the words
to disguise what
i see make
visions palatable color
these words with
a palette more lady
like less blood

in language not mine
that houses no beauty
no comfort for
nature for me
words horrific and terrible

what this shine eye
girl sees through
bars and barbed wire
prisons prime
real estate 25 years
later no escape
2 years before me
attica was auschwitz is algeria
ripped naked and stripped
humanity forced to
crawl mud-like
and 25 years later
war criminals still celebrated
babies consecrated animals

no words there
are no words to

sugar this up
genocide passes as
eye candy for
media hungry for cash
and like cash people are
passed from hand to dirty
hand open palms
passing sand through
time not mine living
on borrowed clocks
          tupac is dead and attica forgotten

in language ugly and time
up where is there space
for flowers
in hearts jailed there are
no morning glories to bid
god a good day
kids lick flames of
hot ice screams
rain stark

where the rainbow arch
to wash eyes
clean of rwanda bosnia
and iraq again
fill mouths with angels'
breath to make forget

memory absorbs like soil
there are no words
and not one word
erases my earth

brothers keep me up

is your skin still soft
here feel mine   a shine of survival

feel   you left me
wet   love dried on thighs still
aching said you were
sore after the last
time   are you still

you broke heart and
out   i still light candles for
your safe journey to
the corner   pray your
flesh won't be too brown
today   your beauty too offensive

    shot for being   a spic around a drunk cop
    lynched for being nigger   loud to klan ears
    deported cause your name   is mohammad and
                      somewhere

    a bomb went off
    drugged up and drunk   cause you native to the
    land and claim birthright

i fear for your life though   no longer in it
wrap a rainbow serpent   round you to keep
harm at arm's length
i charm gods to keep you   safe til revolution is over

    no longer lay beside me and still keep me
    up at night

is your skin still soft
not your fingers' long   strokes or tongue's insistent
welcome keeping me up
     the statistics   political promises that you won't live to see 30

how many incidents since we last kissed

don't believe in this
world ` so i fight
so you'll live to
love free   who you want
i   know that's not
me   so i don't call
don't write   take your
space   your love back
baby   be safe in it
got you
i got your back even
as i watch my own from
the hurt left behind

are you soft still

those who would
kill you   send my way
i'll tell them they
wrong you ain't no boy   you man
enough to get up every
morning despite a reality created   against you
man enough to resist to fight   man enough to break
heart fully and
without looking back

i believe in love and
got my own back

writing this and you don't care. you've moved on and away.
still keep me up.

after us is gone
our temples bombed
people killed
i'll pray for strength and
whether or not i get it
rebuild a chapel   strong
and for good to house
love and freedom
brick by brick   blow
trumpets to herald
our new day

honey   even if we don't
your children and mine will
know each other in   love   in dignity

let them talk
about getting over you
getting over revolution

i believe in love
struggle by day and
sometimes lay
awake at night wondering
if you ever wonder if
my skin is
still soft

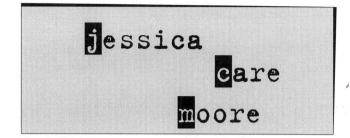

Jessica Care Moore

Motown native Jessica Care Moore attributes her first experiences reading African-American literature to her mother, and reading literature in general to classes in high school. Perhaps most important, Moore's drama instructor, Susan Story, had students perform Ntozake Shange's award-winning play *for colored girls who have considered suicide / when the rainbow is enuf.* Moore says, "I wasn't in the play; this is definitely how I found the poetry section in the library, though." This proved to be a crucial point in her development as a writer and as a person—she'd discovered a poetry that reflected her own life experience. Of this drama, famed as a declaration of independence for young African-American women, Moore states: "Every black girl has seen the play, or has been in the play. After that, Ntozake Shange and other women writers opened up a whole thing for me."

Moore's steadfast objective was to become a journalist, yet her interests went beyond that calling. She was elected president of the Black Students Union at Wayne State University and served on the executive board of Detroit's NAACP. By 1993, she was hosting a reading series for women only at the Pourme Café. Full-time, Moore held down a job as newswriter and associate producer for Fox Television's *Ten O'Clock News.*

Invited to attend her best friend's graduation at New York University, Moore took advantage of the opportunity to visit New York. While her friend's family dined at Sylvia's, Harlem's famed restaurant, Moore investigated an auditioning session next door. Within hours she had a contract to present her poems at an R & B show. Moore returned to Detroit, quit her job, packed some basics, and early in the summer of 1995, took up residency in Fort Greene, Brooklyn. During her first foray into New York's spoken word scene, Last Poet Abiodun Oyewole invited her to the group's show at the Nuyorican Poets Café. (A year before, she had opened for them in Detroit.) She recalls his introduction: "We're going to bring this sister on stage."

Moore received such an enthusiastic response that she sought out another poetry hub, but in her neighborhood. Having walked in on a Friday night open-mic reading at the Brooklyn Moon Café, she admits, "I didn't read the first week because I was too scared. I met poet Tyren Allen because he was the tallest. Eventually, I met Sharrif [Simmons], and kind of figured out who my friends would be." Returning to the Nuyorican Poets Café, she witnessed another poet creating a buzz. "I saw Carl [Hancock Rux] the first time singing. I knew he was a poet, but he was always singing in the Nuyorican. This is what was happening," Moore recalls. "It was just an incredible thing to throw myself into."

Into hip-hop before she ever arrived in New York, Moore also fell into making regular rounds of the clubs that didn't draw the line between rappers, comics, and spoken word performers. Moore sets things straight, saying, "I was doing Caroline's Comedy Club with Hot '97 and Dr. Dre and Ed Lover, because that's where the audience was. I wanted to perform for regular folks, and I didn't necessarily care if academia accepted me or not."

Caught up in the charged ambiance generated by spoken word shows, Jessica Care Moore began performing night after night. Even though there are listings published weekly in major publications and monthly in New York's *Poetry Calendar*, Moore and her posse moved mainly by word of mouth to more "under-

ground" mics. Then, to pay the rent, Moore worked at the *Daily Challenge*, an African-American-owned Brooklyn newspaper. Some five months later, after Moore had fired up a standing-room-only crowd at the Brooklyn Moon Café, she took the phone number to the Apollo Theater offered by a fan. She called Maxine Lewis, who scheduled an audition for "It's Showtime at the Apollo." Moore looks back saying, "Everyone was singing and dancing and I was like, 'I'm going to do a poem. I don't have any music.' I did my 'Statue of Liberty' poem and Maxine pulled me off stage and said, 'Oh, you're bad. I'm gonna put you on.'" Breaking the record for number of appearances, Moore won five consecutive times on this nationally syndicated show.

In the midst of all the subsequent publicity, Moore accepted an invitation to tour the college circuit with the Last Poets. After a 1996 performance for the award-winning musical *Born to Sing Mama* before five thousand young people at Madison Square Garden, Moore realized, "I really need to be selling something. These people want to take a poem home." Representatives from the publishing industry remained aloof, but when they did approach Moore, they suggested that she write fiction "purely for commercial reasons." Angered, Moore wrote the poem "I Bet You Want Me to Write Fiction" and decided to publish her own collection of poems, entitled *The Words Don't Fit in My Mouth*. Empowered with the idea, she decided to found Moore Black Press. A year later, she also published *The Seventh Octave: The Early Writings of Saul Williams*, before Williams became a film star in *Slam*.

Moore says, "I want to promote the poetry of my generation." In this regard, Moore has urged editors of youth and hip-hop magazines to run poetry pages. She told the editors of *Blaze*, "A lot of the hip-hop audience enjoys poetry shows, so put poetry in the ____! magazine." This speech won her a forum in the December/January 1998 issue of the magazine *teeing off* with poet Asha Bandele over the question "Is Poetry Hip Hop?" She quotes mentor Abiodun Oyewole: "Poetry is hip-hop the same way jazz is bebop." Moore herself concludes: "Although one may argue that the lyrical content of poetry is the major thing that differentiates it from rap, it depends on the MC or the poet." Adamantly, Moore also makes clear the integral connection of her writing to activism. "My work comes out of being an activist; it doesn't come out of wanting to be a poet. I was an activist first." Without pause, Moore continues: "Then I've always had this voice. I wanted to be a writer in some form—a novelist, poet, whatever. My poetry developed because I worked on it. It became something I actually cared about." Moore's ambitions segue non-stop one to the next: she wants to record a hip-hop record, she wants more than cameos in film and video, she wants to compile an anthology of women's poetry from around the world to be published by Moore Black Press, and she wants her plays to be staged and then rescripted for the silver screen. Asked if she would ever stop writing, Moore fires back: "No. I would probably die. I have too much inside of me. I would explode."

Miguel Algarín booked Moore's first play, *The Revolution in the Ladies Room*. The Lincoln Center–backed Here Theater, with support from the New Federal Theater, staged her second play, *There Are No Asylums for the Real Crazy Women*. This play demonstrates just how dedicated Moore has been in developing her craft. Jessica Care Moore appears on various spoken word recordings, including a cut on *Here I Stand*, alto saxophonist Antonio Hart's Grammy-nominated CD.

black statue of liberty

I stand still above an island, fist straight in the air
Scar on my face, thick braids in my hair
Battle boots tied, red blood in the tears I've cried.
Tourists fly from all over just to swim near my tide
Or climb up my long flight of stairs.
But they trip on their shoe string lies.
Piece by piece they shipped my body to this country
Now that I'm here, your people don't want me.
I'm a symbol of freedom, but I'm still not free
I suffer from class, race and gender inequality.
I wear a crown of knowledge, 'cause I'm a conscious queen
My mask is one of happiness, though my history here is full of misery.
Done deliberately.
I am America's true statue of liberty.
You placed a bible under my arm, after you ripped me of my faith
And made me pray to a fictional imposter
So, if you were trying to maintain liberty
Too late, you just lost her
'Cause her torch is about to serve as the night light for truth
In the slums and the ghettos that you find so uncouth.
Education will be delivered not from the tree, but the root.
So, little black girls and boys will check their pockets
For spirituality rather than loot
'Cause liberty is just old mother nature
And although you don't love her, she'll never hate ya.
She's earth, wind and fire, don't tempt her to show her power.
Turning all weeds to flowers.
Looking into her wise eyes will make a blind man see
How can you dare name a eurocentric girl after me?
Assata Shakur Barbara Jordan Nikki Giovanni and Angela Davis.

These are the real symbols of liberty
'Cause that stone faced French woman ain't gonna save us.
The same folks who enslaved us.

I'm sitting at the back of the bus, 'cause I feel like it.
And I play ball
Not 'cause you pay me to dunk it, dribble it or hike it.
I'm taking all my people back home, and breaking them mentally free.
I am the walking, talking, breathing, beautiful statue of liberty.
I sweep crack pipes out of school yards
I nurture my man when times are hard.
So, where the hell's my statue?
What's the liberated woman gotta do?
Place my name in wet cement
Every month I pay the rent.
Put my silhouette on a stamp
I'm not a ho, slut or tramp.
My children aren't on crack, and neither am I.
I want to see the words, "Go, strong Black woman,"
When the Goodyear blimp flies by.
I can bake cookies, bear babies, preside over revolutions
Get rings out of tubs, wear a suit, sport baggy jeans, slick my hair back
Or tie it up in braids.
My aura is unafraid.
So, no statue in the big apple can mess with me.
I am the walking, talking, surviving, breathing, beautiful
Black Statue of Liberty.

one afro's blues

I want to feel safe in here
but even the walls know the difference between another woman
and your sista
Sistas call when you think everyone's forgotten
remind you who the hell you are when you just can't seem to
remember this morning
There are times I know I am in exile in Brooklyn
a stranger in a borough of free spirited artists, Black poets
many who think a head of nappy hair means your shit don't stink
or she wouldn't really try to get with your man behind your back
Conscious girls don't do that
Many of our people hide insecurities, issues and mental disease
under layers of limp can't get it up locks
that wouldn't walk alone on my block
where Black folks who work in the community
can't always afford to be lactose intolerant
Breasts full of promise burst and blow Diaspora's dream
inside baby's breath
Decorations around the roses
but never roses
I suppose we could all be among the chosen
but I doubt it
The most prolific
don't sit around writing poems, do they?
Sometimes I see with borrowed eyes
that know much more than I do
Most days I try to yank them from their sockets and push them
inside the holes of someone else's face
Dun calls this morning to encourage me to continue doing my thing
invites me to read at Revolution Books the same evening

He says a woman claiming to know me argues that I said my
inspiration comes from the white side of me
and I'm wondering if this elder sista wakes up with blood on her sheets
if she gets to wear her blackness without question
or is she also betrayed and murdered
like Malcolm
by her own people
When people start saying your full name in intimate circles
your spirit forms a square
crawling on the ceiling afraid to walk among the opinionated leaves
changing color around your feet
Carving out windows at the top of my head
I scream vulgarities, politics, principles, my panty size, and
my oral fetish for pen tops
in the comfort of my own home
I will not define myself with false definitions of survival
There are so many dead pretending to live among us now
So many who wait for the opinion of others before getting out of bed
I recognize sistas hiding in groups of sistas
bonded by foreign letters, colors, class and the fear of loneliness
Women who don't like one another
exchanging false teeth like table salt
Tongues tied to the wet lie licking wounds like
a good humor bomb pop
on a hot day when you read an article in a New York magazine
calling your life-work "that Jessica Care Moore shit"
when I just arrived 24 months ago
Two years of a child's life
I am in exile with my other mothers
slave women who when forced to eat their poems
carved them in the sides of trees
sweat their prose into sheets stained by rape
whispered lyrics into their baby's ears

When conversations start sounding like good hooks
without verses
the song is a lie
even if the track is bangin'
hanging from a wise-tree prophet sizing up of his children's future
Paper cuts
when roots bleed the grass is no longer green
and slavery is the next scene
We all blow up
There are names for those select pieces of poetry pussy
you can only speculate about from afar
and why can't I write about my fertile soil
Are your hands dirty from wishful digging?
Names for those female artists you call girls
biting and blessing the mic, lips spitting up
all the leftover sexy conscious bullshit
from the performance last night
Today I am not the hour glass shape of your political platform
your poetry goddess wearing wrap skirt
star in a cultural video store soft porn
Today even my lips hurt from all the dirt
I eat with dinner
So here we are hiding in this room
like we know one another by last names
pretending we are warriors without pain
Unfortunate truth comes with uncertain fame
I am acting out a positive character in the frame
and I don't know my lines today
so I guess I won't speak to strangers

Most of my comrades—my sistas—don't—
probably won't ever
organize a rally

or wear their culture like a prize you win at a carnival
I lie my body down among
women in exile from themselves
hiding from arms that are supposed to shake
lakes that wait for them to wave
men to secretly save
women who forgave you for not considering them
down with your sisterhood
My girls who balance school, work and kids and actually take a day out
of their week to get their nails and hair done
or feet massaged
that's some real revolutionary shit
Women who may never take their hajj
but will re-create Mecca in a three bedroom brick house
on Detroit's east side
Sistas who nurture themselves better than the holistic bonfire babies
born into what we call community
We are hiding inside the poverty of art
that can make you rich in spirit
but who cares if the people who need you
don't ever hear it
So today my head is not covered and African goddesses
don't recognize me in the light
and I surrender to the woman I really am
in the presence of so many imperfections
claiming to have the answers
with a microphone, music and the background dancers
when the greatest show is never on stage
It is the truth of being alone
about finding at least one woman you can really call sista
in this lifetime
to help you not feel lonely in the garden of apple myths

Women who wipe blood and hypocrites from my fists
farming the poison fruit
churning cocoa butter to cover the permanent scarring
tied in bows around my wrists
resisting a rest
cause there is not time for sleep
I find plain words to be quite deep
I reintroduce myself to people who claim to know me in the street
If you weren't ever a ho
are you sure that you're queen?
Coughing on your crown of new Fort Greene afro sheen
vegan body kinda lean
traveling with pseudo wonder woman power
I'd cut off all your grass roots
and hope to find the blacker flower

i am a work in progress
for Asha Bandele

We are born writing
but will learn to wait
An agonizing line of blood will follow our future
and never find us
mistaking our memories for actual events
reason and common sense will never make an appearance
opening the door after a temporary disappearance
the fisher man showed up in your world again
guess that's why our women heroes got fancy
with addictive names like
Heroine

You were born writing little girl
but you will learn to wait
the lines will appear as currents
events to fool you into submission
the grocery store
the post office
the unemployment line
the local train platform at two in the morning
this where you will find poetry
screaming between the air inside your walk
this is how you'll learn to kiss and paint
nurse babies and call "Next!"
On the ball court
your name will be one African syllable too many
for jane who didn't do her lower case b
phoenix assignment
pretending that she just can't pronounce Kenya or Brendesha
with america's alphabet
this is the moment you find meaning in cuss words

you will take cuts attempting to find the front line
your scent will leave hunters running in the wrong direction
as your home becomes brick your bones become thick
clocks will confuse the moon into thinking
dark is a synonym for gloom
you will stay still as your body leaves the room
for the first time in weeks
strength will appear from behind the sun
they will call you a freak and you will believe them
you were born writing and will soon learn to run

We are born writing
but will learn to wait
the wind will pause our dreams
lies suddenly sound like laughter
we will survive in here or after
skeleton woman break dancing
into poses resembling roses
emulating an african nose
that never smelled ivory up close

This is when you will cry the most
learn to gather your tears into your fists
realizing water will never grant your wishes
reflections are always true but never wet
so we kiss ourselves
till our lips turn dry and honest

You will hear faint pieces of your voice
in the electricity of a phone line
screaming for freedom
in the middle of a message or a voyage
never delivered during long distance
conversations or kidnappings

this the moment your fingers
will find your hand
and hang up on your past beliefs
What is a white courtesy phone?
Why can't I ever find one?

The lines will appear as a sound waving
goodbye
when you jump off the side of the ship
in the footsteps of the march of tears
funeral processions will break into the hustle
digging up murdered soil
that forgot this was a man's world
and daddy needs a son baby
everybody will wear black
forgetting this is your damn birthday party
There was a time we didn't have to wait
nine months for our children to be born
we just believed they would come
and waited for them to quickly leave
I'll take the young pretty one
with the chiseled brown lips
for 5 axes   3 pigs   2 arrows   1 chicken and a bushel of wire

This is when you'll carve your first pencil from wood
and draw blood
this is when your story is erased
I was born writing
but will be taught to wait
I am an incomplete sentence
a work in progress
and I'm not finished yet

there are no asylums
for the real crazy women
an excerpt

Jess: I just want to talk woman to woman, all right? I'm trying to keep your man out of this, but it seems like he's the only way I can get close to you. Guess you already know what I want, huh? I want to tell your story. Your non-story. I mean after 1934, there is almost no record of your writings, only your death certificate. How could a woman with your spirit be reduced to confinement for eleven years without a . . . ?

Viv: (finishing the sentence with venom) FIGHT!!!? What do you define as confinement, dear? Tell me the difference between an artist and a human. One of them knows life is a prison, the other spends their life trying to be free. Which one are you? Tom never left me, he would never leave me. He was just afraid of my protection. He listened to conspiracies. He was a bit weak in that way. So I was always with Tom, see. Why? Why? Why? Why do you need to talk to me? I am not some heroine of history. I haunt literary circles that see poetry as a structured, disciplined art form. Miss Care Moore, you know the people who aspire to be prophets aren't ever prophets. Either one is a poet or one is not. Simple. It's not some choice you make. It's not a course you study at a university. It's a life that chooses you. It's up to you to accept, of course. And, I don't. Accept, that is. I never did. So, I don't need or want your help now. I'm not to be treated as a child in my death as I was in my life—a damsel in distress. How dare you come to me with your '90s womanist jargon and expect me to carry the banner for the cause. The madwoman's club. The poets' wives club, the "I was married to a famous man that left me" society. I am sure this would only bring more shame to the *royal* Eliot name. What is

wrong? What is missing? Tom would never tell me. Maybe you
will. Do you know where he is?

Jess: Usually at Barnes and Noble in the poetry section. Why are
you asking about Tom? You can't get the man to talk to you in the
afterlife, damn, why do you think I can. This isn't about him any-
way. Look, I'm not trying to get you to join anything. I want the
same answers you want. I want people to know you weren't some
crazed woman with no control. You are an artist, and by defini-
tion, psychiatry still considers the creative mind as a mental disor-
der, labeling "feverish brilliance" as a manic phase of craziness.
Vision redefined as hallucinations. Neurotic. Even Tom is accused
of being psychotic. Words like assume, suggest, could, think, pro-
pose, perhaps, probably, took your life. Left you to die alone. Your
poetry unpublished. Your husband lost forever. Girl, being in love
is insane. So we are all guilty. There's Vivien Leigh, messed up by
psychotropic drugs. What about Judy Garland? Or Billie Holiday?
Valium, Ritalin and Thorazine, I went to school with all these
girls! These chemical straitjackets for women with skills. Viv, I
know you love Tom, but your rebellion against the so-called
morals of the times makes you a female experiment in the mental
hygiene movement (that means brainwashing) whether you like to
or not. So, what's up, Viv, are you with me?

ishah

attached to strangers
who smell like family on Sunday morning
you'll never really be loved that way again
this shit is temporary
keep reminding yourself baby girl
while looking for unconditional daddy love
that he will only have his eyes
but never his heart
will have his walk
but never his feet
we are born in battle creek searching for
ourselves inside the weak
so we can appear strong
entertaining confusion on canvas
unfinished colors   reminds me of my brother
woman who wonder   when they get to turn into
a seductive action figure
invisible planes   flying
little girls learn to summon the rain
when tears dirty their face and their dreams start lying
sleep bandits stole your sight
you never gonna know how to love right
cause your heart is on the left
your spirit's mistress wants back in
but your body is locked inside its first life
you've been labeled ho, mother, wife
where's my gold dipped knife my sacrificial womb
oppressed bone buried in stretch limo tombs
opening the door the way gentlemen do
we'll have a table for two

but only one of us is gonna eat
you think I look beautiful when I sleep
my skin melted to the floor
while I was counting sheep
so I keep one black eye open
hide my power inside my throat
swallow when necessary
talk too damn much and practice whispering
tell you my secrets then ask you to protect me
from the truth
you are my best friend
my nigga my motha fucka my boy
hurting me like my man would
I never knew love like this
I never knew pain like this
my daddy was a fish
but scorpions don't like to swim
unless they're drowning
it's more passionate that way
we love because we have to
not because it's practical
or matches the curtains / goes with my new dress / looks good in
pictures / sounds good off the page / works for the soundtrack / makes other
people feel tingly inside / or just because we happened to both be
standing here
when the perfect music came on
and we knew how to dance without practice
remember baby girl
he will have his eyes
but never his heart
he will have his walk
but never his feet

still
you will stand on his shoes
close your eyes and pray this time
that if it's not him again
at least you will know
you came close

mirrors

Am I still woman with one breast gone?
Hanging around one man too long
legs give in to knees I can't locate
Was it my spirit I ate when I cooked you dinner?
I try angles still the mirror is always square
stare cross-eyed so sometimes I can see two of me

laughing at myself
crying for no one else

I am looking for the man in me
trying to figure out why that second syllable
was attached to my womb   and

Today my body has no room for visitors, freeloaders or lovers
my frame holds fingerprints from being moved hanged on nails
                    displayed on white walls for decoration
          I see you looking in me trying to find sanity in vanity
                         while combing through your hair
                    I break in pieces just to fuck with you
          so you will think of me for seven more years
                    even if you're not good looking

Today I pressed my one breast against the glass / cut off one arm
                    bit off my one good bottom lip   and
                         kissed myself the way you did
                    when I was considered woman
                         bearer of children and water

My blood no longer colors the moon
No sperm will find a name
and I notice how woman it must be
to feel
Just like a man

tracie morris

brooklyn-born Tracie Morris states that she is a poet, not a singer. While this is true, she is clearly a musical poet influenced by jazz, blues, rock 'n' roll, hip-hop, funk, avant garde, Afro-Cuban music, and spirituals. Morris is a poet who uniquely works a tune to hip-hop rhythms in a bluesy way. Within her narratives, she accents syllables in relationship to the beat, but with superb timing and a verbal velocity characteristic of hip-hop freestyling or jazz scatting. She is adept at layering internal and end rhymes as well. Often accompanied by musicians, she recites in sync over articulated rhythms, something musicians appreciate. She knows how to drive the momentum of a poem, or even a set. Since 1991, her unique style has brought her marquee gigs on stages featuring poetry, music, theater, and dance. While her poems seem to literally skip across the page, the wonder of her performances is the sheer speed with which she enunciates her puns, enjambs her syllables, and syncopates her phrasing. This form is not new; it's ancient among the verbal tricksters. The Greeks called this kind of patter without pause *pignos*, a double-quick delivery that leaves one out of breath. Obviously, Morris can keep pace with MCs, or any professional auctioneer for that matter. Amazingly, a poem's savvy insights, fresh in code and lingo, are never sacrificed by the speed of delivery. For all this, Morris epitomizes the spoken word artist.

Morris sat in on one of her first jazz collaborations just like any musician new to a scene. Steve Coleman and the Five Elements were playing at the old Knitting Factory. As leaders typically do between sets, Coleman asked Morris if she wanted to perform. Of the experience, Morris observes, "You know, he is notorious for his odd time signatures, so when I finished sitting in with him, I knew I could hang a little bit with musicians." She concludes, "If I could get through this baptism by fire, I could pretty much play with anybody."

With this feather in her twists, she went on to perform poetry with D. D. Jackson, Badal Roy, David Murray, Graham Haynes, Kevin Bruce Harris, Leon Parker, Donald Byrd, Mark Gilmore, Marvin Sewall, Greg Osby, Mark Batson, and composer/conductionist Butch Morris. Either they invited Morris to join in on their gigs, or she's called on them to back her for her own concerts. She has also sat in with Kelvyn Bell amd Grammy Award–winning vocalist Cassandra Wilson. Morris often works with Vernon Reid, and she notes that this collaboration "involves more sound poetry." She says, "It has a much more theoretical framework in terms of how music and words interact."

Reflecting on her craft as a poet and as a musician, Morris says, "I think of the instruments as speaking, and I'm having a conversation with them." While working on a commission to provide lyrics for choreographer Ralph Lemon's *Geography Project*, Morris realized that no matter what it's termed she works within language, oral and written, even though, as she points out, "I am in the musicians' union. I consider myself a writer [who] talks with instruments." Morris is also a member of the American Society of Composers, Authors, and Publishers (ASCAP).

The music world has not always been kind to Morris. She went to a Living Color concert in 1989 and lost her first collection of poems, a journal, passport, and personal address book in the vicinity of a mosh pit. She recalls: "All my tickets to the outside world were lost, and I couldn't write for two years. . . . I just kept thinking, my best [work] is gone; I'm never going to remember this stuff." Morris did write again and went on to win the Nuyorican Grand Slam Championship in 1993.

For two years, Morris hosted the Monday night open-mic readings at St. Mark's Poetry Project in the East Village in Manhattan. Full-time poet Morris has performed in England, Switzerland, Germany, Denmark, Korea, and Japan, and has toured extensively throughout the United States. She has recently recorded with Emily XYZ on her *Take What You Can Live* (she is co-poet vocalist on "If They Don't Get It"), Elliot Sharp on *Time Bomb*, Leon Parker on *Awakening*, and Graham Haynes on *Tones for the 21st Century*. Morris also appears on the compilations *Nuyorican Symphony* and the *Best of the National Poetry Slam*. Her poems are included in the anthologies *360 Degrees: A Revolution of Black Poets*, edited by Kalamu Ya Salaam and Kwame Alexander; *The United States of Poetry*, compiled by Joshua Blum and others; *Rock She Wrote: Women Write about Rock, Pop, and Rap*, edited by Evelyn McDonnell and Ann Powers; *In Defense of Mumia*, edited by S. E. Anderson and Tony Medina; *Soul: Black Power, Politics and Pleasure*, edited by Monique Guillory and Richard C. Greene; and *Aloud: Voices from the Nuyorican Poets Café*, edited by Miguel Algarín and Bob Holman. Morris's collections of poetry include *Chap-T-her Won* and *Intermission*. Besides winning the 1993 National Haiku Slam, she received a New York Foundation for the Arts Poetry Fellowship. Morris leads werdz-n-muse, a seven-piece band, and teaches a course in performance poetry at Sarah Lawrence College.

switchettes (las brujitas)

bubble, bubble
toil and double
dutch too much
turning into trouble

tapping time til
we just can't take it
chanting rhymes when
moments make it

blessed and cursed
being double handed
leaning to left
strands deftly commanded

understudies be understanding
switchettes fidget digits
turning dispel, casting
breaking curses

portal dimensions
simple phrases
making mischief
not to be phased as
bracelets clink

in sync thinking
sweethearts' names
invocations through
games and—

> *. . . tell me the name of* _____
> *k-i-s-s-i-n* _____
> *Miss Lucy had a* _____
> *saw James Brown sitting in the gutter . . .*

even when Ali needed mo' machismo
he put dopes on the rope with a
butterfly float, flippant wrist
let loose noose's grip

like we girls did
reworking the kinetics
left-turn, right-turn
over-hand aesthetics

feet doing double-time
meter reason school's
in season, flip in, flouncing
guild's lilies

dust clouds breezes
ten little drummers
summon up old stories
speak in tongues

old souls buster's shoes
got the blues and browns
round white fronts
tassels flat down

keeping up chatter
through patter
in the 'pation
vibes 'verberating

teeny-bopper nation
tensile strength
making it stand
knot still yet grand

Significadence
ain't random
We clasp our hands
in tandem

private service announcement

Tracie don't do no druggin'. You must be buggin'. Not even a gambler is she. Stays away from the blunt and the budda, The 40's, the liquor. Don't chug-a-lug the OE.

They slowly poisoning my brain. Got to train it to keep focused as is. Without jamming, I mean slaving to the pipe or weed or the coke or the dope or downing gallons of beer fizz.

So . . . what do I do for recreation? Contemplation on my text is just one type of messing I do. Writing is cool. Truly moves me. Groovy. Don't get enough of it. Just hanging tough in it.

Love is the drug that I savor. Rare if the flavor that can make me tingle. But it's the liquid of love when it mingles that's the flyest kinda of high you can bring to the table.

No fabled knight of armor necessary to get the best of me. I'm self-sufficient, see. Don't depend on men for money just honey from the sweet nectar of life when one spends the night.

Sometimes admit I'm shy and downright frightened. So I keep both eyes on who I spend my time with. A night room with some bright gloom from a candle lighted. Excited 'cause quality's high but numbers so low. Don't like quick drips from a slick rick or deputies who come, droop along, then doze. Solely someone I love, okay, *like* a lot only gets me hot or access to the spot.

Make me climb the rafters so I wouldn't need to swing. Do it right, not a fling, a one-to-one thing. Flirted with freaking, it

didn't work. Not a sparkle but a spurt. Next time I'll get a soda
if I want a jerk.

Turn to the point when the connection's right   it's magnetic. May
be slow   to start but   very very energetic. It's pathetic. Folks
think that   lighting or   drinking the right   things or   the white
thing can really get them going.

No . . . I dress up for the occasion. Lingerie or to the T. Modesty
makes for investigation. You can wear   a thong or   a sack   jack,
nude's   cool   but have the   cap black,   so there won't be   no
distractions. Love ya brother but don't know where ya been or in
who   and won't   be offended   if those   thoughts vis-a-vis   me ran
through you.

After we've dispensed with the formalities, reality of the situation
is at hand. I'm every woman, you can be the man.

I plan to make the evening wonderful. Under it   all, thresholds
fall   joy's   in tandem. The connection and feeling's vibing hope
You're lively 'cause believe it I'm   not a dud, Love. It's the drug.
The Thrill of the moment. No   smoke foment or ferment from
rocks or by barley and hops. (Which may delude you to think ya
doing good, but a stiff board sitting in liquid usually softens
up the wood.)

My final point succinctly, is   Love's   so cheap,   it's free. Per-
fected over centuries, legal between adult people. Alternative
therapy   relieves tension   locked in   makes a better bond. (And
when he's working the boot knocking   There's no hurry if its jock
unlike jumbos there's no worries 'bout him going through your
pockets.)

So, yes. I'm clean living, nope to the dope. Being sharp wanting to act smart only trying to cope. "When it's time to relax   one thing   stands clear . . ." it's my man here   and   he needs   some attention. I've extended myself a little high time   gonna get mine with some affection and my brand of special blending.

writers' delight

My writers delight
in meta (1-2-3-) 4.
Score with words.
Activist verbiage rounds
out primordial sounds.

My writers display
back in the day,
snake charming
voracious contemplation.

Fade to black smack dab
in history.
Mysterious back draft
liquid consistency.

Word smitherine tongue
curls quilling the silence /
Nommo sounds empower their
nether surroundings.

Pounding shores up heartbeat
simile metronome.
Like *guaguancó* berimbau
gospel sounds and home.

Jambalaya jamming
sounds black to me.
Like a take it higher
in a jazz soliloquy.

Rocking rap Fats sang
blue musical thrills.
Void fills Hendrix'
little wing.
Decoy that's willing /
Tripping the tip of
a cacophonous swill.

Chilling words think
I vampirically drink.
My feat the ink
extending my kind's line.
Binded in mind.
Timeless memories
tick-tock-tick.
Quicksand shifts
land mass to see.

Improvising on a
Miles Trane melody.
Nat Duke Turner Cole
freedom rings.

Swing the shoutout
Sound waves loud.
Pushing the envelope
moving the crowd.

Fiercely proud.
Judah lion cuddles cubs.
Words and music big up
Reggae dub.

Pride of crews' rep
liberating in clubs.
Wielding weight of
each generation.

Sanctimonious promise of
a hosted nation.
Notions of potent and
splendid reflection.

On the strength continuum
links up connections.

Engulfing sonic
revolutionaries
eclectic vision.

The rhythm
the rhythm
the rhythm
must be on
a mission.

life saver

Congolene free SG
Dap sans dax. Unkneaded
He's so so savvy!
On bright, but no shine

Replace the Ha (cha cha cha)
Trade the happy
for the dreaded N

Seentcha flicka
(tag: He of the Sunshine
Sammy genus)

So, Junior, betta watcha step
when they start acksing:
"How many, uh, can ya
count the culluds?
Didn't Fred and Kelly, er, ra, ah
bust ya move?"

"Nah, Mista see,
thas no steel life.
Bubba's bunioned
blistered & bludgeoned
even mo' on the one
twernt cut, um, runnin'."

Drummin' up biznis
y'all said we cain't
be playin'. Pickin' on feats
Call in a Toe Jam. Baby.

Little man buck dance
Bruva decking halls
G-Lover hit off missives
Metal of Honor on point
—tow, heal, toe

Mistaken shuffle ain't slow
flow's constant staccato.
That boot black front
bubbled up for *somethin'*

Spit on spirit slavin
the one container

So pure he floats.
Heir is buoyant
like a life saver.

step

To the
beat
down size

polyrhythmic
glut, just
sound off.

Strut,
military time.
Intricate chimes
Canes shout
suits & pounds.

Greek
bloods let
spring in
fertile
African ground.

Hit it
with a bang
or band.

Timberlands
hightops translate
Azanian
bootstraps.

No taps,
trudged
warriors souls

Goal to communicate
middle
pass-age.

Roll call.
Fall in line.
Show time.

Snap sharp
for atten
tion!

Dare one mention
the synchronicity?
At ease?
Don't be
deceived by simplicity.
Collective spirit
bigger than the hole.

Got soul.
Bros & sis
clicking their heels

appeal to
group's good,

and go
home.

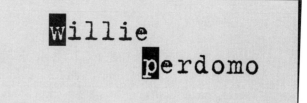

Willie Perdomo

It's no accident that Willie Perdomo's most anthologized poem, "Nigger-Reecan Blues," is dedicated to the man who wrote the classic memoir *Down These Mean Streets* some three decades ago about Perdomo's own neighborhood. Triumphantly, Piri Thomas's unsparing depiction of his adolescence in New York's El Barrio defies a society that cruelly rejects his Nuyorican, Spanish, and Puerto Rican heritage with its slave and African past. The first line of Perdomo's "Nigger-Reecan Blues" asks, "Hey, Willie. What are you, man? *Boricua? Moreno? Que?*" Victorious in his own right, Perdomo not only has an answer, but proclaims it in his work.

Even before Perdomo knew the alphabet, he authored books. He recalls: "I used to mark zigzag lines horizontally on eight-and-a-half by eleven paper, one row after the other. I was going through the physical action of writing. I'd stop after I had a whole stack of papers." Early on, Perdomo enjoyed the sensation of holding a manuscript, and he was anxious to create a text in his own name.

Perdomo's parents arrived in New York from Bayamón and Ponce during the migration of the late 1950s. Between the time he was born and when he first headed off to P.S. 96, Perdomo's parents separated. His mother had noticed his talents, and additional validation came from his earliest teachers. Matter-of-factly,

Perdomo relates: "I was always on those accelerated tracks in public schools. I was reading at a high level, my math scores were high, but not as high as my reading, because I really took to books." While the discourse at home continued to be in Spanish, at school it was English-only. Valuing his early exposure to both languages, Perdomo continues to read, write, and speak in Spanish.

By the fifth grade, Perdomo relates, "I had a teacher who just saw it in me and she gave me some applications." The "it" stands for Perdomo's prodigious talents. He received a tuition scholarship from the Friends Seminary, founded by Quakers, on East Sixteenth Street—more than one hundred blocks from home. Of this experience, Perdomo concedes: "It was really weird, I was trying so much to be like these kids in prep school . . . and at the same time I was being ridiculed by my friends uptown. I didn't really know where I fit. I'd always feel like this monkey in the middle." Ed Randolph, the receptionist then at the Friends Seminary, put things in perspective. Perdomo relates: "He told me I was special. It was hard at first because I was torn. I'd go to school and I'd be reminded of where I was from. Yet, every day I'd get off at 125th Street. I wanted to belong in both places."

Perdomo received other scholarships to attend summer camps outside the city. Writing was the way that mother and son stayed in touch. Perdomo notes, "She always sent me letters and wanted me to answer them." He adds, "My mother kept journals. If I went off to camp, she'd write, 'My son wrote me today.'" Not everything was conflict-free. Perdomo had to learn some hard lessons.

Perdomo describes one such lesson Ed Randolph taught him after a fight at school: "He put me in a headlock and said relax. He told me that this kid's father could have me thrown out of school the next day because he was paying and I wasn't. The second thing he told me was to redirect this energy I had."

Soon after, Randolph invited the eighth-grader to a poetry reading at a school assembly. Perdomo reflects: "He just started reading this beautiful poem about him and a friend during the Vietnam War. It wasn't that the friend passed away, but that he came back unstable, and didn't recognize Ed." Continuing, Perdomo underscores the associations that the poem evoked: "I started to think about my friends. There was no war impending, but there was a connection and the language was so real, it spoke to the experience. I said, 'Wow!' That got me to the point where I wanted to write poetry." Perdomo continues: "Maybe this is what he meant when he said, 'You have to do something else with this energy. You have to be creative with it.'" Not only was Ed Randolph's reading the first occasion that Perdomo heard poetry spoken, but, he emphasizes, "I actually felt it to the core." At this moment, Perdomo was struck with the realization that he truly could express his emotions without paying the consequences of a battle he would ultimately lose because of social structures beyond his control.

Soon thereafter, Perdomo had his own day in an assembly. He went up on stage, and, he says, "dressed in my blazer, my tie, my slacks. I read a couple of poems. Afterwards, a math teacher came up to me with tears in her eyes because I had touched her." Perdomo says, "Right off, I saw the power of the word, and how words have powers to create emotions in others."

Under Ed Randolph's tutelage, Perdomo expanded the range of his reading. He recalls: "The first two books Ed gave to me to read were *The World of Apples* by John Cheever, who is one of my favorites, and *Leaf Storm and Other Stories* by Gabriel García Márquez. Then he started to turn me on to the sixties and the black poetry movement. I read Amiri Baraka, Sonia Sanchez, Haki R. Madhubuti—those writers."

Once, on a mission to purchase books for a class, Perdomo went to Barnes & Noble. He remembers: "I'm walking by and turn my head. I see *Selected Poems* by Langston Hughes, and he's on the cover. I look at it and I say, 'Wow! What's this?' When I began to read all the references to Harlem, I said, 'Wow! Wow!' It wasn't required reading, but I put it on my list anyway. I went home and I read it." Perdomo states that this opened him up to a new chapter in his self-perception and nascent aspirations. "I fell in love with the medium," Perdomo declares. "I thought it was powerful and efficient at the same time. In other words, even in short poems, you can read a lot into them. Hughes was economical with the language. I think just in terms of time, this form of writing is efficient."

During the early nineties, Perdomo often read his poems at the Nuyorican Poets Café and was one of the early Grand Slam Champs. At present, Perdomo still roams the spoken word circuit, but his literary aspirations steer him toward a resolve that he recognizes in his favorite writers. Perdomo crafts his poems for both performance and publishing. After all, by reading in public, Perdomo builds up a demand for his forthcoming books.

Perdomo's accumulating manuscripts include a memoir-in-progress and a multigenre narrative of prose and poems entitled *Stop Signs*. His first collection, *Where a Nickel Costs a Dime*, is accompanied by a CD. Perdomo's poems appear in the anthologies *Boricuas: Influential Puerto Rican Writing*, edited by Roberto Santiago; and *Aloud: Voices from the Nuyorican Poets Café*, edited by Miguel Algarín and Bob Holman. He was featured in the PBS specials *Words in Your Face* and *The United States of Poetry*; the latter was also published as an illustrated art book. Besides being recorded on the CD compilation *Flippin the Script: Rap Meets Poetry*, Perdomo has appeared on BBC radio and TV. In 1997, Perdomo cowrote the script of *Spicy City* for HBO. In 1997, Perdomo was runner-up in the Poetry Society of America's first book award. Currently, Perdomo works for a New York publishing house.

notes for a slow jam

This is the poem
you always wanted
I've turned into
a fire-can crooner
to sing you this
slow jam
a farewell greeting
no sooner than the sun
set on our meeting
I had a song for you
but first
I had to sample
from the midnight
quiet storm
break up to make up and
make up to break up and
break up to wake up!
I was a three-time loser
persistent fell in
heart over head
not even a chance
to carve the initials
of our romance
on the bark of a tree

There was nothing
no one left
to point at
and say
"it's all because of you"

so I have an encounter session
with the bathroom mirror
the black crescents
that real makeup
under my eyes
couldn't cover
the cries
of walking down the street
falling off the peak
of a broken heart binge
had to get high
so I buy a bag
to cure my love jones
and soothe my aching bones
I walked into a social club
and found the answer
boiling in the juke box—
pick a song—
hip-hoppin' through life
I used to think that salsa
was just for the rice and beans
I was wrong
it's a remedy for those
strung-out love fiends
Would you think I was high
if I told you that Tito Rojas
was a Greek playwright?
I'm saying that Euripides
sang salsa
for real
check it out
the tragic hero
is chillin' on the corner
love epics and shit

spillin' from his mouth
the chorus
is on the rooftop
giving echo to his pain
listen to the sound
of a heart breaking

> *aye aye aye*
> *aye aye aye*
> *y dicen que los hombres*
> *nunca nunca nunca*
> *deben lloran*

> *and they say that*
> *the men*
> *should never never*
> *cry*

I look into the mirror
one more time
before I chase you away
and just in case
you don't speak Spanish
I leave you sinking
into some muddy waters

> *you can't spend what you ain't got*
> *you can't lose what you ain't never had*

My pockets are empty
and I'm letting you go
without a fight
but before you go
here's the poem
you always wanted

reflections on the metro north
Part II, Spring 1997

Monday morning
and I'm on the 11:10 a.m.
From Poughkeepsie to Grand Central
and I ain't running away
from anything
I said
I'm not running away
from anything
I'm on my way
to see Judge Alderberg
with a letter letting him know
that I went to go
tell it on a mountain
and that I don't have to be
locked in a cell
to find myself

The sun is bouncing off
this updated reflection
and as the doors close
the steam whispers
I start singing

> *I'm starting all over again*
> *It's gonna be rough—so rough*
> *and tough*
> *but I'm gonna make it*

Believe it or not
this is the ride of my life
like the seagulls skipping on the Hudson

I know where the wind
is taking me these days
I look out the window
sure that the sun
is following me
that the big house on the hill
will one day be mine
so many nights
I rode on this train
with my Harlem princess
sleeping on my shoulder
wishing I could start over
in between Garrison and Peekskill
where ducks dance in the street

The walls of Sing-Sing
play a song in electrocuted time
and locked up minds
this is no tourist attraction
had my life stood on the express
this would have been my stop

The blue pin-stripe banker
has an office sitting on his lap
making the Big Apple spin
from his seat
he is getting richer
from stop to stop
I want him to hear this poem
to understand the bliss
of not needing a bag of junk
to see through the abyss
of ill wind

By the time we reach Yonkers
my belly starts to bubble
I used to think it was enough
to celebrate
the salsa of *mi gente*
but Miky said it right
when he said
I say it in Spanish
I say it in English
there ain't nothin' new in New York
mira me pana
no hay na nuevo in Nueva York
the boogie down Bronx
is not burnt or broken
they building blocks
for the future
but my shit
is still kicking up
cuz I'm getting closer
to El Barrio
my belly flip-flops
belly flip-flops
land of smoke shops
death in hip-hops
black justice
at the hands of
white cops

Remember brother remember
if you don't remember
you are doomed to repeat
remember
the poems you

used to write
about the block
where dead-end
screams are heard
too late
and everybody
turns the other way
this is
home
125th St.

Brother, brother, brother
there're far too many of you dying

The doors close
the steam whispers
a slow ohhh shit
look at those two
four-door Tauruses
parked by Park Avenue
TNT is eight deep
they're about to jump
on a direct sale
don't sleep
to be aware
is to survive
signals are in sync
from corner to corner
moves the dope seller
my old fortune-teller
sticking and moving
Look Mr. Banker
that ain't me

no more
123rd St.
where I sold dope
for breakfast
ran from the police
and pawned my passport
that's where I
used to shit

There's my building
on 122nd St.
where I learned
to say good morning
to Miss Mary

where I used to
kneel and pray
in front of
San Lazáro
San Martín y
Santa Barbara
that's where I
used to eat

This elevated view
is good enough for me
ain't nothin' new to dive in
cuz there's a thin line
between you having to die
for me to live

Before I get to Grand Central
the core of this strange fruit
I start a prayer

God, grant me the serenity to accept
the things I cannot change

and stash the peace
I found

Grand Central Station
so fast
make sure you remember
to take your personal belongings
and leave the past
where it belongs
it's time to put
the bass in my bop
no more selling my soul
to the highest bidder
everything is entertainment
safe and clean
I saw myself dying
on the corner today
but the sun was shining
and I started singing

> *I'm starting all over again*
> *It's gonna be rough—so rough*
> *and tough*
> *Sooo rough & tough*
> *But I'm gonna make it*

haiku

In recovery
Every day speaks to my soul
Today I'm alive

stop signs

This poem was born
the night we rode
the Tube to Brixton
somewhere between
laughing and crying
It could have been
the A train to the Bronx
but the stars
in the magazine
would have said
the same thing

> *I have to finish what I start*
> *A romantic decision is hard to make*

I'm not sure
how one is supposed
to read the stars
unless they're falling
all over you
In London
it would be hard
to read through the fog
people walk in the rain
even if they're not
in love
If it was up to me
I would grab the ones
that shoot across the sky
shak'em hard one time

blow on them for good luck
and let them roll
see what they land on

> *apuñala mi corazón*
> *con tu cuchilla de amor*
> *mi amor*

It's proof
you're my angel
I'm ready
to love again
In Piccadilly Circus
Eros is pointing
the wrong way
If you look for rain
you will find
gold muses
in the middle
of a rooftop
swan dive
Those damn swans
I remember them so cool
shooting up into schools
of six
and I said maybe
I should leave her a note
before my flight
thanking her
for giving birth
to this poem
that came oozing
out of the crack

down the middle
of my heart
Her Spanish
was good, too

     Hablas Español
     Sí
     Te amo
     Y yo te amo también

She danced salsa
better than me
I called her *mami*
by mistake
even though she told me
that she ain't into that
papi thing
you know
that *aye papi si papi*
si papi tuyo papi toito
I said it's okay
I wanna call you
honey sugar sweetheart
baby boo

So far I've painted three pictures
sung five songs
but the only time
I see her
is when my eyes
are closed

Gotta catch myself
before I get hurt
so I flip the script
one time

If you can be with the one you love
Don't love the one you're with

I was ready
to leave those
dark hallways frozen
in yesterday's rain
but I must leave soon
so I wrote this poem
because it's
the only place
where this love
can live

carl hancock rux

In June 1998, following the publication of his first book of poetry, *Pagan Operetta*, *The Village Voice* heralded Carl Hancock Rux as one among eight "Writers on the Verge of Shaking the Literary Landscape." One might say that Rux was on the verge sometime before. When he was seven, after a trip to the Liberation Bookstore in Harlem, his foster mother gave him *Selected Poems* by Langston Hughes and prophetically inscribed it: "To Carl, you are a writer." Reared as an only child (his biological brothers were adopted by other families), Rux escaped into the world of literature. By the age of nine he had read James Baldwin's *Giovanni's Room*, Jean Genet's *The Blacks: A Clown Show*, and Aimé Césaire's *Return to My Native Land*. All the while, he was writing and illustrating short stories and poems.

Rux recalls his adoptive parents opening up their Saturday night bar to play jazz and tell stories of prewar Harlem. Predictably, the references and rhythms worked their way into Rux's texts. "They would play King Pleasure, Nat 'King' Cole, Lester Young, Miles Davis, Dizzy Gillespie, John Coltrane, Gene Ammons, Dinah Washington, and Billie Holiday," Rux notes affectionately. "They gave me lectures. 'Listen to the chord progressions, listen to the phrasing.' I must've been eight years old." He concludes: "It stayed with me—the idea of music and phrasing. I'm sure this influenced how I approach writing and performing verse."

Recognition of his talent came first at the High School of Music and Art, when the Xerox Corporation selected Rux to be

included in the Harlem Writers Workshop, a privately funded three-year journalism program conducted on the Columbia University campus. After high school, he entered Columbia, but in 1989, Rux's older brother, with whom he had been reunited briefly, entered an advanced stage of AIDS and Rux became his primary caretaker. He says: "That experience, of finding then losing my brother, opened something up in me. Identity became a crucial theme."

Shortly after his brother's death, Rux wrote a drama inspired by the ordeal. His *Song of Sad Young Men*, a play with dialogue in verse to be accompanied by a live jazz band, was produced Off-Broadway in 1990. It made its way to the National Black Theater Festival in North Carolina, the ETA Creative Arts Center in Chicago, the American Church of Paris, and then, adapted, it went to the National Institute for the Arts in Côte d'Ivoire, West Africa, and on a U.S. tour. This play propelled Rux into a professional career he'd only dreamed of previously.

After Rux finished at Columbia, he entered the Sorbonne in Paris to study comparative literature. He admits, "I wanted to find Claude McKay and Richard Wright in Montmartre. I went looking for people who weren't there because they'd been dead for fifty years." He continues: "It's really funny to look back and see that Paris was not available to me the way I expected it to be in 1991. It wasn't the refuge where all the great artists sat in cafés and discussed art and literature."

Returning to New York, he began working in theater with composers, dancers, and installation artists. "I became interested in how other mediums inspired my text." Miguel Algarín produced Rux's *Chapter & Verse*, a poetic narrative with movement and a cappella vocals at the Nuyorican Poets Café. The play was produced later at The Actor's Playhouse in Greenwich Village. Pursuing his investigation of various mediums, Rux arrived at the University of Ghana to study with the National Theater and

Dance Company. Rux observes: "There, I discovered more than dance and drumming to poetry. The economic crisis, politics, conflicts among cultures and religions, as well as the AIDS epidemic in West Africa, further focused my perspective." Summing up the experience, Rux says, "Writing and performing was not some novelty act; spoken word, movement, and music were presented as rituals true to traditional forms of expression."

Shortly after returning to the United States in 1992, he was a corecipient of a "Bessie," the New York Dance Theater Award, for a collaboration with Lisa Jones, composer Alva Rogers, and Rent choreographer Marlies Yearby. He was also awarded the Nuyorican Poet's Café's 1995 Fresh Poet Prize. Rux was on his way to perform poetry at the Berlin Jazz Festival when he was named one of "Thirty Artists under the Age of Thirty Most Likely to Influence Culture" by The New York Times Magazine. Rux later traveled to Hong Kong, Bali, and Singapore as a commissioned poet with Jawole Zollar's Urban Bush Women Dance Company. He was invited to be resident artist at the Ebenezor Experimental Theater Lab in Lulea, Sweden, and he was also commissioned to write and perform his poetry for the Alvin Ailey American Dance Theater. Rux appears on Alvin Ailey American Dance Theater: Revelations and a Musical Retrospective of 40 Years of Dance.

His poetry, plays, and fiction appear in numerous anthologies, including Action: The Nuyorican Poets Café Theater Festival; Plays, Monologues, and Performance Pieces, and Aloud: Voices from the Nuyorican Poets Café, edited by Miguel Algarín and Bob Holman; Go the Way Your Blood Beats, An Anthology of African American Fiction, edited by Sean Stewart and E. Lynn Harris; Soul: Black Power, Politics and Pleasure, edited by Monique Guillory and Richard C. Greene; Fire and Spirit: African American Poetry; Korper Lust Sprache, a literary journal in Berlin; Poetry on Stage, edited by Regie Cabico and others; Beyond the Frontier, edited by E. Ethelbert Miller; and Poetry Nation: A North American Anthology of

Fusion Poetry, edited by Regie Cabico and Todd Swift. Rux's poems and essays have been published in *Essence, Paper, Interview,* and *Shade* magazines as well as *The New York Times, The Village Voice,* and *L' Express* (France). He appeared in PBS's 1997 documentary *Shattering the Silences,* was the subject of two documentaries produced in France, and has performed on CDs including *Eargasms* and Reg E. Gaines's *Sweeper Don't Clean My Streets.* His own CD, *Rux Revue (Sony 550 Music),* was coproduced by the Dust Brothers. Forthcoming are Rux's first novel, *Asphalt,* and a play commissioned by director George C. Wolfe for the Joseph Papp Public Theater.

the excavation

Within four walls and one window
an acreage of shore stretched black and five feet deep
beneath a standing lamp, a desk, a chair—
Fragments of Treasure Buried posted where the sky should be
ceramic pieces springing up from its borders
quieting itself, growing without the merit of
the bougainvillea or the frangipani flower—shards of things
slicing the tissue of clumsy walking
long lines of blood streaked between rows of found objects
culled carelessly.

He bled once, in the early years before he
knew how to harvest the crop of things personal
when he reached out and took hold of cognizance with both hands
surprised
ripping tendon and severing bone back into the soil—
new treasure, these pieces of himself—swallowed.
The cultivating required maps and field songs in season
before investigating clay
where prayers were hidden
and dolls slept without their heads—
even forgotten gestures
a certain light cast at a certain angle and recipes for trembling
had been laid to rest here.
These things were not to be disturbed without prostration.

There! Keep digging!
His directive to the faithful,
a cell phone at his ear, sanguine silk suit caked in dry aubergine
fax machine vomiting wax sheets, computer screen providing

all the light there is,
and hands and hands and hands, delving.
Requests come in
for anything specific to all things hallowed (and even what does *not*
     belong to him):
Saliva stains on pillowcases, sunday evening headlines,
reactions tied to responses connected to what was felt
at certain moments in certain places
where windows were curtained with ochre
and aloe leaves had been embroidered at the hemlines—
requests for everything fear obliged.
Against the northern wall, boxes are stamped for shipment
and tightly packed while the faithful, still on their knees
with magnifying glasses (and a guideline for questions),
skim away at top layers with delicate spoons
listening for bits of laughter and conversation out of context.
He points *There! There! There!*
and obeys imposed silences when fresh graves are exhumed.

At some hour these walls will faint away
when the undaunting command is not forthcoming
and his will to retrieve no longer surpasses his will to resolve.
Then, in the eviction of diggers, the quake of walls and the death
     of requests
only the stage this plot of land is heaped upon
will remain . . . unearthed.

blue candy

Boy has candy Blue candy   Grandmother loves candy
Boy shares blue candy with Grandmother   Blue candy
Boy is four Boy is four and unkempt Grandmother is fat Grandmother is
fat and unkempt   The apartment is a railroad Grandmother is sleeping
Grandmother has blue candy   Loves
candy Blue candy   Loves blue candy on her tongue
Grandmother's tongue blue   Grandmother's lips blue
blue lips are open blue tongue is sleeping
Grandmother is blue and asleep
The apartment is a railroad
A railroad that smells of stink   Grandmother is fat
and smells of stink
Grandmother is asleep in blue stink
Grandmother   you make *axdent*
Grandmother is asleep   Make *axdent* on herself
Boy is in apartment with blue candy naked
Grandmother is in apartment with blue lips asleep
Grandmother is asleep

Girl cousin lives with Boy and Grandmother in stink railroad
Girl cousin got cat woman glasses fixed with tape
Girl cousin plays with dolls   Girl cousin and dolls are not at home
Uncle Eddie lives with Boy and Grandmother and Girl cousin
in stink railroad   Uncle Eddie got bubble hands and sleepy eyes
Uncle Eddie plays with Boy's body and needles
Uncle Eddie and needles are not at home

Miss Lady from hallway plays with Grandmother   sometimes
Grandmother and Miss Lady from hallway play with cards
and bottle in brown bag   Miss Lady from hallway knocks on door

Miss Lady from hallway got bottle in brown bag and cards
Miss Lady Hallway comes to play with Grandmother
Boy talks to Miss Lady from behind locked door
Grandmother has candy   Blue candy
Grandmother is asleep   Grandmother make *axdent*
Make *axdent* on herself
Grandmother loves blue candy   Grandmother is blue
Grandmother is asleep in blue stink

Blue men with shiny buttons and red light
make noise outside window   Blue men with shiny buttons
bang on locked door   Break locked door open   Blue
men with shiny buttons open broken door   Blue
men in door look like blue
men on TV Dragon net   Grandmother is asleep
Shhh
Dragon net men with shiny buttons who break door open   poke
and push blue Grandmother   Grandmother is blue and stinks
Blue men give naked boy a T-shirt
and marbles with different colors on tin board   Marbles make star
on board   Board has holes for marbles   Put marbles in holes
Different colors in different holes
People are outside   People outside come inside   Inside
apartment   Apartment is a railroad that stinks with windows
People talk loud and open windows from inside   Red lights outside
windows blink on and off   Red lights outside come inside   windows
and blink on walls
On and off
Everything inside railroad is red   Everything is red inside railroad
apartment   Different color marbles   turn red on and off   Blue men
all turn red   Grandmother must be cold   Blue   cold   Red and blue
men cover Grandmother with dirty pink sheet from bed
Grandmother make *axdent* on bed

Axdent on pink sheet bed   Grandmother is covered in dirty pink
axdent sheet
Grandmother's feet are showing   Feet must be cold   All people inside
railroad talk loud   Miss Lady Hallway talk loud   Miss Lady Hallway is
crying Blue   me   Shiny Buttons talk loud to Miss Lady Hallway
Shhh
Don't wake Grandmother   Grandmother be mad

Uncle Eddie is here now   Uncle Eddie look sleepy   People talk
loud to Uncle Eddie   You want to play needles   Uncle Eddie?
Girl Cousin is here now Girl Cousin is in her good coat and hat
glasses fixed with tape People in railroad take Girl cousin outside
Uh-oh!   Forgot her dolls
Girl Cousin   you want to play dolls?
Woman with shiny black bangs and curls sits next to Boy
You want to play marbles?
Black Bangs and Curls plays marbles with Boy
Man in green hat stands next to Black Bangs and Curls
Black Bangs and Curls smells nice   Green Hat man says nothing
Black Bangs and Curls   is that your name?   Boy asks
My name is Arsula, woman with shiny black bangs and curls says
Arrrsoooolaaaa Boy says   That's a funny name   I got blue candy
Arrrsoooolaaaa   Grandmother loves blue candy Grandmother
make *axdent*   Make *axdent* on herself   Grandmother is asleep
Grandmother is asleep long time   Cold blue sleep on pink *axdent* sheet
You want some blue candy   Arrrsoooolaaaa?

Blue candy on my fingers   Blue candy around my mouth
Blue candy mouth   Blue mouth like Grandmother
Sorry, Boy says no more blue candy for Arrrsoooolaaa
No blue candy for you
Boy?   Black Bangs and Curls asks
Would you like to come home with me?

Man in green hat says nothing

Boy has shiny marbles and blue candy fingers
Red lights outside window make everything red inside
railroad   All people inside red railroad talk too loud
Shhh
Grandmother is asleep in blue
Grandmother make *axdent*   Make *axdent* on herself
Shhh   Grandmother is asleep in blue.

The yellow car is warm

suite repose
an excerpt

I think Archie Shepp played *hambone hambone where you been* in our living room the night faces & fists melded mellifluous melancholy madness onto red river carpeting—spurt, splash, torrent falls, gushing reds, primeval screams crashing through vodka spittle, sharp tenor sax and subjective alto, trumpet, trombone, hambone bass and Roger Blank drums . . . blank . . . drums . . . blank . . . Shepp's lyricism lurking behind ficus and forlorn fruit and rhythm patterns lined in gold fringe, clutched / clutched in our living room, in

Where you been? Arrangements scattered from kidney-shaped cherry wood coffee table and Camels sleeping in red river woven carpeting, caravans of Camels and Kools and vodka and blood and Shepp and rhythm . . . I think Garvey's ghost came to play with me between Charlie Brown sheets to the percussion of belt buckle slaps and cracked wall mirrors and ripped chinese watercolors, or was it *Mendacity?* Either way, the party was in my pillow, where cutouts held court with *Right On!* magazine centerfolds. Conversation was had, freely—and maybe Junior Walker interrupted for a moment, or might have been, then again—

I think, it was . . . no, yes, it was *Mendacity*, it was Abbey Lincoln who sent herself into my restlessness and jazz frenzy and comic book high and quivering and quake and not sure now what the silences mean after Johnnie Walker Black Black Black came crashing down to the harmonic freedom and improvisation of Roach and Mingus and Hawkins and Dizzy . . . Dizzy . . . dizziness . . .

. . . they don't tell you about this in record jackets, what to expect when Booker Little sings on that trumpet, when Carlos Valdéz gets to *cong cong conga-ing* the beat to beat to beat the beat the beating taking place in the circle of frenzy, in your living room, and there are no sequins for this diva . . . no boas, no rhinestone tiaras, no pencil-black eyebrows arched in pride across her forehead, or gentle shadows softly sleeping above the lid of her falling eye, her falling eye in sweet repose, no straightened hair illuminating lights and gels and gobos, not in your living room . . . just Charles Tolliver's *Plight* to her modern dance ballet; *ronde de jam* of the knee, to the fall, to the fist, straight back, and lip split side turn (ever so gracefully, ever so soft) and hard and swing and bop! And bam! And pow! And Dizzy . . . Dizzy . . . dizziness . . . swelling cheeks . . . weak alto sax . . . strong bass . . .

elmina blues (cobalt through azure)
an excerpt

(There is a prostitute in Nkrumah Circle)

Her carrion:
>damp
>shiny
>bulbous-black
>dusky dirt
>painted earth of
>eyes and dead of
>night.

Hill of
>iridescence
>lips and lid
>of colors
>dun, dark, darken.

Impervious face
>of mirrored earth
>thick
>Kohl-black
>wash of pink
>and red and baby blue pale
>across the terrain
>of obscurity.

Smooth face
>inviting earth
>quake and quiver
>of cheek and

      sucking lips
      eclipse of lash
      and rising brow.

White
      hands
      marauding
her dusky earth
      nipples
wedged between her fingers
white
faint fingers touching
crevice of land
      black
      inviting earth.

Milwaukee white
      hands
King's English hands
milky white
      fingers
fingers pallid
      cold
bleached hands
      traveling
frost moving
across
sable
      penumbra
sooty
      dark
resplendent
      earth.

She leans in with knees crossed and toes crammed in heels. Fake ore of gold, foreign and fashioned into something of nothing, lynched and hanging from her lobes. Imitation stones of paste catching no light, dead, buried above the ground of her hands, no light, dead on third finger. German Rastafari leans in, touches ass and sips gin from her bottom lip. Blond roots meshed into sickly turds of apple green. Tresses falling over shoulder, caught in bulbous constellation. Red. Black. Green. Thread entwined and roped around his waist, pale, sickly blue eyes and blond lashes, marauding her neck and thighs and shiny ass, then leaving change, consuming last of beer, and taking hand—and taking her, away from Nkrumah Circle, through crowd of vendors and kerosene light, from the sound of yelling voices and open call, up the road, on foot, foot on terra-cotta soil, to tiny field, not far away, out of the circle, just left of here.

On foot. Foot on earth. Earth in his hands,
and
finger in
then lay it down
and pull it up and
bend it down and
rend the veil
the veil twain
pallid stake
pushed into
dusky earth
and steady
motion
and rock
and
roll!

And
Mother Land
is on her knees
frosty fingers
in
fake gold
swinging off
corpses from
ancient ears
and
nothing like this,
dark and wet
and smelly too
on Mainstein Strasse
or cobbled hill.

Blonde snakes fall over face and now stand up, saliva
mouth, and scrotum breath, now on two feet, feet on the ground,
terra-cotta soil, and open hand receives the bills, and folds them
into a shoe and she smooths back her plastered locks, fried and
sheened, and spits out the taste of pubic hair . . . then returns to
the circle
where we wait . . .
We wait our turn . . .
To reclaim this land.

kuta near seminyak

Down to the lip of the water
offering something to the Goddess

The elements congregate
where conception is. Where
everything is born,
          The air
            climbs up
through
the openings, I bow
legs entwined in holy water,

above the stir of vanity
Her frame became unrecognizable
against white foam visitors rolling in

face wet
feet covered in sand,
a silver gift
hurling itself into
an undulating brine
          mighty water
riding a welcoming wave
that pulls itself back into the abyss

Kissing the mouth of Denpasar
the brandishing current—
I cursed the greediness of a billowing upsurge—taking
flesh and bone
blood and foam—
and cursed the robbery of tithes

and then I watched her form promenade its way back to me
toward the beach
coming in
from an even line
that merged with that scrim of darkness
White foam folly replicating an early morning turn
(nakedness curling around my feet)
pulling from my shoulders and waist an urban trajectory . . . too familiar
(nipples caressing spinal curve)

rise spirit rise!

She washed my face with languid kisses,
then rolled herself back out
pulling soil from between my toes
remnants of Bali in the fists of the Goddess
an incandescence furbishing between blue fingers
the lyric of the ghost emanating from a briny depth
laughing then
at the absurdity of this (my nudity) and

years of crossing trenches to see the other side of things—
yes . . . to know faces without lips

The mountains have not known me this way
the tenements with their secret apartments
have never noticed the details of my feet

This is even more than I've ever known about myself

the sound that comes from my throat
when I am surrendering to ocean currents, rejoicing at my endurance.

untitled

excerpt, for Miguel Algarín

(His bell when pushed does not return sound
just a little amplified voice on
Second Street after a while inquiring.
My mouth against the thing.)

It's me . . .
I am in love . . .
I am downstairs standing on a landmark . . .

I've been sleeping for three days and three nights on benches
splintering my flesh
in the company of supine angels
sipping cups of grog
inviting me to peruse wide margins. Latitude. Space
where vagrants walk in the direction of nowhere descending
toward nothing . . .

And when we approached a dense coppice of trees
recalling tenses
transcribed two hundred years before now . . . I leaned
in the optics
of those branches that centuries are quick glances
viewed from blind peripherals
and what the leaves cannot see—they listen to . . . and keep as
sacred mementos
until the next thing becomes the marker of time . . .

Everything has fallen from my pockets . . .

All the prayer beads and monologues of sage
All the pages decorated in silver poppies
All the things half cast in moonlight and molten sweat
All the bushwomen's dances
All the sounds of a horn ever made toward the breasts of barfly virgins
All the witches with decadent eyebrows painted anything but blue
All the maps tattooed for mother in constellation configurations
All the pianos pulled out to make room for bass lines and screams
All the vacuums filled rhythmically
All the chances to know resolve
All the political agendas of the criminally insane
         inspiring me to know . . . everything has fallen away

I'm standing downstairs
in the company of Baudelaire's corpses
drinking with me: The Angel of Longing
and the Soldier of Epoch
and the Judge of Discontent
and the Captain of Amphetamine
in the company of sentiment

We are drunk with self indulgence
We have not recovered from death
We are infected with romanticism
We are consumed with notions of
a politicism and South Bronx tragedies

Come down
(wisdom and folly are meaningless)
the city has been tightly shut
it requires an ark to be carried
by a dying poet armed for battle . . .

An uncircumcised archer
of arrows anointed from first cry
lives in Brooklyn
with his languid bride—
she is covered in paint and mandrakes,
their firstborn

yet unredeemed . . . and the pedestrians are
murdering him with applause
(murderous congratulatories)
come down and sever his ear so he
can survive his hands (all is trouble)
come down and take out his tongue
so he cannot sing his father's sermons

He is called Saul, his voice is beautiful
hear it? & leave it there
we are captives of the gospel
he and I
we are still escaping Jesus
we sing together sometimes from
disparate places . . . we are young and all is
trouble . . .

I have found a southern priestess
laughing with blues theory ingredients
of conjure . . . a holy whore regarding a
foul organ hidden behind her breast
that betrays the pulsing of blood and
the motion of air
her waist is a hill of fruit falling into
a bed of *floris et vaginae magnitudo*
and her virgin boy

keeps watch composing
sonnets until she can walk
out onto the plaza and raise a banner
for Marie Laveau

She is called Tish:
her work is complete in incompletion
and her bed is beautiful and verdant
you should see her
you should see her feet
her feet are charming with earrings
her garments are proud in colors
her hands are crowded with amber
come down and set her chariot
amongst the royals
so she can pick her teeth in the
courtyard of anointed temples
and decorate the interiors with
saffron and aloes

Come down and see
we are young and dwell in
gardens with too many contestants
we are unfinished and live in rooms
without enough instructors
we are aging and chosen and
poorly trained for mass redemption

Everything has fallen away

Your breath is strong with drink
your eyes are bright with fatalities
the cleanliness of unscarred pages

grows from your scalp
let the children write commandments
in your hair.

It's me
I am downstairs
I have no pleasure
I am in love
stop my youth . . .

(His bell says nothing when pushed
his small amplified voice is groggy
is grandiloquent
is sleeping
then silent
then nothing
save what he said on page.)

© Robert Hughie

mariahadessa ekere tallie

reading at the Brooklyn Moon Café, among other spots in Brooklyn, Tallie not only began to invoke feminist themes, but developed them beyond the poem into monologues, which then became performance pieces. She cofounded Words and Waistbeads, a six-woman collective that performs poetry and prose to music and dance against sets prepared by one of their members who is a visual artist. The multigenre works are intended to stimulate discourse among members of the audience. The purpose of these performance pieces is to encourage women to create changes in their lives.

Tallie's feminism does not rehash the issues of the seventies; rather, she exposes the complicitous nature of passivity and how some crimes committed against women may be obscured by the guise of custom. Tallie also challenges larger social injustices by illuminating how they affect the most intimate of relationships. Still, many of her poems are simply love poems, and by their dedications, serve as mementos in the way that snapshots do.

Tallie sees her immediate goals clearly. She looks forward to the next phase of her life. She muses, "I want people to know my name as an excellent writer." Then she adds: "I want to feel about my writing the way I feel about Ntozake Shange's writing. You know?"

Born and raised in Queens, New York, Tallie has developed a passion for traveling, which she indulges in frequently. She likes London, but she's not partial to cities. Returning from a small town in Holland where she attended a writers' workshop in 1998, Tallie remarked, "You know I'm a country girl." Tallie is planning on moving to the "country," meaning "far from New York," to work on her M.A. in creative writing—credentials she wants for dual careers in teaching and writing.

With this ambition long in mind, Tallie has been an apprenticing writer since youth. She attached her first poem to a Christmas tree; subsequently, her parents gave her an orange plastic typewriter that aided the flow of poems. That her parents "kept a lot of books in the house" provided further inspiration.

During high school, on her own and in defiance of the staid curriculum, Tallie discovered Langston Hughes, Maya Angelou, Nikki Giovanni, and Alice Walker. With some pride, she reports this, noting, "Alice Walker was a very big influence on me; I read all of her books. Around that time, I decided I was going to be a writer." As a college student, when Tallie sent poems to Ira Jones in St. Louis, he accepted some for *Eyeball,* his poetry journal, but not without the advice, "Read more, write more."

When Tallie returned to New York after graduation, she attended her first poetry reading. She recalls, "I saw a sign that read, 'Poetry Reading: African Voices.'" She adds: "I noticed Sharrif Simmons, who was hosting the reading. I'd met him when I was in high school 'cause he worked at the Liberation Bookstore and I was always there." Tallie continues, "He said, 'I'm having a poetry workshop. Why don't you come?'" On the occasion of the poetry reading, Tallie introduced herself to Carolyn Butts, publisher of *African Voices.* After a brief conversation, Butts offered her a job. In time, she became a senior editor. From this initiation into the spoken word scene, Tallie had a workshop to go to and a job as a writer. By June 1995, she says, "I was reading every Friday at the

Brooklyn Moon Café." This is when Tallie returned to the books of Ntozake Shange and others.

Tallie's poems have been published in the anthologies *Catch the Fire!!!*, edited by Derrick I. Gilbert and Tony Medina, and *Beyond the Frontier*, edited by E. Ethelbert Miller. Her poetry has also appeared in *The Atlanta Bulletin*, *African Voices*, *Long Shot*, *BOMB*, *New Millennium*, *The Shield*, and *Eyeball*. As a journalist, Tallie has contributed features to *Black Elegance* and *Black Enterprise* magazines.

barefoot stroll

I want to walk barefoot
in a place where barefoot has no name
in a place where soul on Earth
is natural
a place where toes in soil
is common as
true love
laughter
and birth.

I want to walk barefoot
in the hills of a hidden holy land
and stare at sunsets with people who
know sunrise isn't guaranteed
in a place where the evening news speaks of tides,
the waning moon and rainforests wild as Oya's dance
in a place where shoe and umbrella are curse words
where dahlias and pearls adorn every head.

I want to walk barefoot
in cities without streets
where admiration is a deep silence
and conversations are replaced by the eloquence of eyes
barefoot in a place
where excuses are not enforced in law books
where there is no law
only that which is right.

When these places leave tracks
I follow their footsteps

but they always lead to the sands
of my own spirit
I stand in the middle of myself
bowing to the Mecca I know
the sight of me
strolling barefoot
into my own life
leaving behind thieves and tyrants
trying to control it.

forced entry

i

He broke into me
stole something
a brazen thief
never charged with forced entry
because "Please don't" didn't lead to
blue black marks on the lock
and no one sees the bruise prints
                    the scratch marks
on my spirit
these don't make police reports
the dignity missing from my step
doesn't qualify as physical evidence.

ii

I shake when I see him
only my homegirls seem to notice
their golden light protective around me
his boys' mantra is "lying bitch"
they mutter it with sharp machete eyes
occasionally someone rouses himself to say it
"Lying bitch!"
the words weigh down the wings of airborne birds
and for the first time
I see these men not as men
but as terrorists in training
camouflaged bombers on the
ground floor of truth
taking dynamite
to its foundation.

I see myself as a prisoner of war
in exile
a survivor
I wish this wasn't my story
but it is
a million times over
and just when I think it has gone away
it reappears at my doorstep
in another woman's face
or on the 10 o'clock news
and although I have loved men since
maybe another sister can't
so this is our story
and it will be ours
until we don't have to claim it anymore
until women from Brooklyn to Oakland to South Africa
can sit back in amazement and say
"I can't believe such things ever occurred."
Until the word "rape"
can be wiped out from our vocabularies
removed from the dictionary
until then, this will be our story
and wounded eyes will tell it
even when we don't.

evolution

i

Potpourri   time traveling mommas
doing somersaults in infinity's playground
jumping rope at light speed
our playmates:
mothers   sisters   lovers
from long ago.
In girlhood
we are unbound.

ii

The world chains us
binds our blood and swollen breasts
to heavy links of
what we can
and can not do
weighs down ankles
cramps
disturbs
our playful equilibrium.
Falling teetering rocking
reaching for baby dolls with one arm
boys with another
who / what / where am I?

iii

Some places
womanhood is
voluptuous attitude
hands full of hips
arms akimbo
in others it's

polite table manners
voices that never rise
teacups and pinkies
it's walking the water path
mashing yam
growing cassava
braiding hair
beading the initiation necklaces
it's knowing the stitch well
spinning sunrise on the loom
it's hennaed hands
red saris
it's bound feet
polygamy
sons over daughters
womanhood is a dirge
and a celebration.

iv
We could be fulla ourselves
and our dreams again
hear the tap tap tap
rope kiss
concrete yielding sound.
Jumping over
girls, jumping over . . .
until something grounds us
saying we are women,
and we can not.
We could be fulla ourselves again
our dreams again,
do the unthinkable
be eternal
unbound.

elemental sounds
Ode to John Coltrane

There's a corner in
heaven where Coltrane solos
are pressed into the
grooves of clouds. Sun rays
sharpen themselves like hands
on phonographs, the
sky spins and baptizes Earth
in a shower of D minor. There is Coltrane
music in my hair, there's a
new song drenching the
tuneless, barren streets. Listen,
it's raining rhythm.

sometimes
for F. B.

and even
with the words
I get lonely.
Poems crawl into bed with me
wrap themselves
around my legs
insistent that they get written
joyous, not having to inch between
a lover and me
stanzas sleep wherever I do
the words more consistent
than any man has been
and still,
I get lonely
between the commas,
before the first line,
after the last
I need someone to
kiss me and the poems
gather us together
in loving arms
affirm us
the way we
affirm ourselves.
Being strong leaves me weary
being soft and loving
the hardest journey of all,
me and the poems
the words more consistent
than any man

syllables sneak up on me
I dream they are you
I get lonely
even with the words
sometimes.

recollect

Remember you, me
ankle to ankle
iron ripping wrists
breaking bones
back against back
in bilge on racks
against ship walls
and walls of them.

Remember you, ripped
from me, ripped
an infant torn from my breast
our flesh
hanging from trees
split skin rotting on our backs.

Remember babies born
not yours
those rights torn nightly from
my screaming thighs
and now the call for my demise
is dubbed tradition.

Sister turns against sister
my mother holds me down
while I howl
wrenching in pain longer than history.

White hands used to force me open
brown hands now stitch me closed

I am a tight hole
a gift to be torn open repeatedly
a mouth without a tongue
woman without lips
my clit has been clipped
my smile has been stolen.

Who will claim herself woman
and sing my song?
Who will mourn my unclaimed laughter?
In the midst of a joyous ritual
will someone
perform a new ceremony for this
skinless, soundless drum
denied her melody
by tradition?

Who will reclaim her voice
to eulogize?
Who will remember me?

domino effect

She knew she hated him
when his fist turned the lights off in her mind.
"He's crazy," her heart hissed in between astonished beats.
Where his voice went
blood and blows followed
always said he believed in giving 100 percent.

There were few signs
             outbursts were rare
now he wanted to fight
drag her hundred pound ass out in the street
screams doubled as gunshots
to the ears of girls who once believed in love
like she does still—
so she's surprised at the intensity of her rage, at his rage
while the babies stand in the doorway and SCREAM
but God has turned the music way up
and she's got to make a MOVE!
he says, pushing her into a wall.
When she looks so confused
it turns him on
where will she go with blackened eyes
and split lips?
It no longer matters.

It's only important she
collect her wits, blot the blood
and tend her babies

before strength becomes a foreign language
and violence, the only tongue she knows.

She knew love wasn't supposed to be like this
for her babies
she won't forget.

distance's destination

Maybe
Marvin Gaye wrote
"Distant Lover"
about you and me.
Your eyes take me in
blink me out.
I see worlds in your eyes
pretty places
you won't invite me to.
I'm ready to explore you
discover us
ready to unravel myself
dive deep / Olokun for you
but you're not anywhere close
and the faraway eyes
prove it.

I recollect myself
stop searching the skin
for the scent of familiarity
consider the characteristics
of a foreigner
and retreat to the source
of my own solitude
and even though you watch me
you don't seem to notice
I'm changing destinations
buying a one-way ticket
out of the past
flying nonstop into the future.

I've got places to go to
and sleeping with strangers
I've decided
is counterproductive.

Maybe one day you'll snooze
in my guest room or laugh
at the way things used to be
or, I'll smell the honeysuckle
returning to your skin
but I can't speculate on such matters
I've got a life to build
thoughts to pack
and a plane to catch.

serenade

You pour red-wine kisses
into my palms
brush copper stardust
across my shoulders
You are a man in the
deep, forgotten sense of the word
opening yourself to the doctrine of surrender
releasing the need to create laws
or force the lotus open for yourself
You meditate on rose petals
listen to clouds
shift in the sky
Man in the deep
forgotten sense of the word
whose walk
is a prayer to movement
whose voice
pays homage to sound
roots to soil
your hand in mine
Our voices entangled
in whisper and sighs
Man whose aura emulates air
you are a wind chime
      in the loud madness
          in the face of what manhood is mistaken to be

a woman's poetic

It's writing
despite the facts
the manmade
facts that say your
language
is sister to gibberish
kin to the nonsensical.
It's speaking over
the clamor of pots
and dishes
it's speaking louder
than voices of doubt
it's stanzas written over ads
in "women's" magazines
it's verses scribbled on
infinite "to do" lists.
It's nursing
broken hearts
with ink.
It's writing
despite the facts
to create new ones.

height

Like bamboo
I only look fragile
bend,
but do not break
sway dangerously close to
the ground in painful angles
do not break
stand straight
stretch high
face closer to the sun
this time
hair tangling up the stars
this time
do not break
do not merely
bounce back
bend
low
and not always graceful
but taller
always taller
when I choose to stand again.

Saul Stacey Williams

"My mother is a teacher and my father is a preacher," states Saul Stacey Williams. In a classic case of understatement, Williams adds, "They set good examples." His mother worked as a multicultural specialist in the Newburgh, New York, public school system and was a member of the Hudson Valley Freedom Theater. His father, a Baptist minister, had his son reciting his first rhymes at church-sponsored antidrug rallies.

Quite responsible at twelve years old and already focused on his talents, Williams received the support of his parents to commute on weekends for acting lessons at HB Studio in Manhattan. Williams enjoys recalling, "Earle Hyman taught Shakespeare there. I would see him in the hallway and think, 'Wow! There's Bill Cosby's father from *The Cosby Show.*'"

By the time Williams entered junior high school, he was devoting his lunch hours to rhyming battles. At home he systematically composed new rhymes to ready himself for the challenges that awaited him. While Williams became enamored with rap at this stage of his life, many influences of the middle-class community in which he lived prevailed. While Williams admired a few rappers enough to borrow the rhythms, he was determined to make rap's form his own. Now, if the press refers to Williams as a "rap poet," he is quick to assert the identity he wants for himself: "I'm a poet. I'm an actor. I'm interested in music." Williams

© ROBERT HUGHIE

emphasizes that he has advanced his poetic forms beyond those he experimented with during his junior high school years. In the meantime, Williams attended classes at the American Academy of Dramatic Arts to sharpen his thespian skills. At sixteen, Williams traveled to Brazil. He sums up the experience saying, "That changed my life . . . so much clarity came."

Williams utilized that clarity to plan his future. At Morehouse College in Atlanta, Georgia, Williams delved deeper into the details of Paul Robeson's life. Williams saw the parallels between his own development and Robeson's. He took counsel from the fact that Robeson had been the son of a minister (and runaway slave) and a schoolteacher. When women in Minister Williams's church told Saul, "Oh, you're going to be a reverend, just like your daddy," Williams retorted, "No, definitely not." Partly inspired by the fact that Robeson had earned a law degree, Williams decided that he would get his B.A. at Morehouse and then study law.

In college everything progressed as Williams had imagined, almost. With a double-major in philosophy and drama, Williams discovered that writing essays in English composition was fun. He finished his assignments promptly in order to have time to write. When Williams became acquainted with other students who were fond of writing, they teamed up to start *Red Clay* magazine. In his senior year, Williams became so seriously involved in writing and theater that he reversed his decision to go to law school.

Studying dramatic arts at New York University, Williams had various professors who required that he keep a journal. By the fall of 1994, he noticed that his journal "was getting to be pretty interesting." He had been writing poems and fragments of poetry mixed in with the required observations. Williams made his debut on the New York poetry scene by reading his verse at a Black History Month event in February 1995.

By this time, Saul Williams resided in Brooklyn. He was

walking on Fulton Street—he remembers precisely that it was on March 16, 1995—when he encountered a crowd in front of the Brooklyn Moon Café. Revisiting the scene, Williams notes that T'Kalla, whom he had met at the February reading, was there. "T'Kalla encouraged me to get on stage," Williams reports. "I did 'Amethyst Rocks' with all my heart, and that was it. The same night I must have met one hundred people and booked ten shows." Williams sums up the significance of what happened by saying, "It was like I was being introduced to a new family of sorts." T'Kalla learned that Williams worked at the Edge City Café and introduced him to Carl Hancock Rux, a regular there. Speaking of Rux, Williams muses, "Reciting, he just blew me away."

Williams pursued courses in dramatic arts by day while he began to make the rounds of the underground poetry scene at night. This full-throttle lifestyle did not prevent him from earning his M.F.A. from New York University's Graduate Acting Program in 1997. During the same period, Williams became one of the Brooklyn Moon Café's "star" poets, who functioned as a support group for each other.

Then, as now, Williams preferred reciting at readings to slamming. As the Portland Festival demonstrated, slams often tend toward slapstick and stand-up comedy more than the art of poetry. Serious about the tradition of poetry and alert to being labeled, Williams says, "I hate to be simply classified as a rapper." He points out: "I've performed at the Brooklyn Museum, the American Craft Museum, and Boston's Museum of Fine Arts. I've performed at the Whitney Museum one night and opened for a rap group the next." Williams wants it to be known that wherever he recites poetry, he does so in such a way that "it won't be classified." His desire for self-definition speaks; he reacts strongly to any attempts at labeling him or his poetry. "That's another thing that can plague us," he says.

Explaining his method of preparation, in particular for younger audiences, Williams says, "I know I have to do something rhythmic. . . It only takes eight bars. By then, I have their attention." Ever developing, Williams divulges, "Sound has become interesting to me. I've started to write songs." Facing the decisions he would make before he ever entered the studio—his debut recording appeared in 1999—he took into account recordings of recent years. "I've never heard a spoken word album that I really liked," he says. Then he mentions his admiration for Charles Mingus's *Let My Children Hear Music* and "The Haitian Fight Song." He also cites Jim Morrison as an influence before concluding: "I have to approach musicianship. I won't do my poetry with music in the background."

Williams appears on the recorded compilations of *Lyricist's Lounge, Black Whole Styles, Eargasms, Deaf Music,* and *Spoken Melodies.* Featured on the sound track to *Slam,* Saul Williams costars with Sonja Sohn and Bönz Malone; he also cowrote the screenplay with director Marc Levin. *Slam* won the Grand Jury Prize at the 1998 Sundance Film Festival and Caméra d'Or Prix du Public at the Cannes Film Festival. For his acting in *Slam,* Williams received the Independent Feature Project's Gotham/Perry Ellis Breakthrough Award. Williams can also be seen performing on *Underground Voices,* the short black-and-white documentary by Reg E. Gaines. Poems by Saul Williams appear in *Slam,* the companion book to the film, edited by Richard Stratton and Kim Wozencraft; *In Defense of Mumia,* edited by S. E. Anderson and Tony Medina; and *Catch the Fire!!!,* edited by Derrick I. Gilbert and Tony Medina; as well as in the journals *African Voices, BOMB, Red Clay,* and *New Word.* Williams's first book of poems, *The Seventh Octave,* was followed by *She.*

gypsy girl

and she doesn't want to press charges
my yellow cousin
ghost of a gypsy
drunk off the wine of pressed grapes
repressed screams
of sun shriveled raisins
and their dreams
interrupted
by a manhood deferred

Will she ever sober?
Or will they keep handing her glasses
overflowing with the burden of knowing?

I never knew
never knew it would haunt me
the ghost of a little girl
in the desolate mansion
of my manhood

I'm a man, now
and then I remember
that I have been charged
by one million volts of change

Will the ghost of that little girl
ever meet my little girl?
She's one now
she must have been three then
maybe four

she's eighteen now
I'm twenty-five now
I must have been twelve then
my mother said he was in his thirties

and she's not pressing charges
although she's been indicted
and I can't blame her
I can't calm her
I want to calm her

I want to call him names
but only mine seems to fit
"come on, let's see if it fits"
two little boys
with a magic marker
marked her
and it won't come out
"they put it in me"
"no we didn't"
"what are you talking about?"
"it's not permanent"
"it will come out when you wash it"
damn maybe it was permanent
'cause I can't forget
and I hope she don't remember

maybe magic marked her
lord, I hope he don't pull no dead rabbits out of that hat
What she gonna do then?
And what was Mary's story?

The story of a little girl
a brother

and couch
she's got a brother
a couch
a sister locked in a bedroom
and a mother on vacation
lord, don't let her fall asleep
her brother's got keys to her dreams
he keeps them on a chain
that now cuffs his wrists together
mommy doesn't believe he did it
but he's left footprints
on the insides of his sister's eyelids
and they've learned to walk without him
and haunt her daily prayers
and if you run your fingers
ever so softly on her inner thigh
she'll stop you
having branded your fingertips
with the footprints of her brother
the disbelief of her mother
and her sister who called her a slut for sleeping

lord, I've known sleeping women

women who've slept for lives at a time
on sunny afternoons
and purple evenings
women who sleep sound
and live silently
some dreams never to be heard of again

I've known sleeping women

and have learned to tiptoe into their aroma
and caress myself
they've taught me how to sleep
having swallowed the moon
sleep til midafternoon
and yearn for the silence of night
to sleep sound once again

painters of the wind
who know to open the windows
before closing their eyes
finding glory in the palette of their dreams

she had no dreams that night
the windows had been closed
the worlds of her subconscious suffocated
and bled
rivers of unanticipated shivers and sounds
that were not sleep

she was sound asleep
and he came silently
it wasn't the sun in her eyes
nor the noise of children en route to school
she woke to the swollen rays of an ingrown sun
fungused
that stung more than it burned:
a saddened school en route to children
who dared to sleep on a couch
exposed to the schizophrenic brother
only to wake with a new personality
one that doesn't trust as much as it used to
and wears life jackets into romantic relationships
can't stand the touch of fingertips

damn, was that marker permanent?
I hope she don't press charges

I hope they don't press no more grapes into wine
because she might get drunk again
and fall asleep

Rise and Shine
my mother used to say
pulling back the clouds of covers
that warmed our night
but the fleshy shadows
of that moonless night
stored the venom in its fangs
to extinguish the sun

Rise and Shine

but how can I?
When I have crusted cloud configurations
pasted to my thighs
and snow covered mountains in my memories
they peak into my daily mode
and structure my moments
they hide in the corners of my smile
and in the shadows of my laughter
they've stuffed my pillows
with the overexposed reels of ABC after-school specials
and the feathers of woodpeckers
that bore hollows into the rings of time
and now ring my eyes
and have stumped the withered trunk of who I am

I must re member
my hands have been tied behind the back
of another day
if only I could have them long enough
to dig up my feet which have been planted
in the soiled sheets
of a harvest that only hate could reap

I keep trying to forget
but I must re member
to gather the severed continents
of a self once whole
before they plant flags
and boundary my destiny
push down the warted mountains
that blemish this soiled soul
before the valleys of my conscience
get the best of me
I'll need a passport
just to simply reach the rest of me
a vaccination
for a lesser god's bleak history

children of the night

i

. . . and out of the Sun's gates come little girls in dresses of fires,
wearing pigtails of braided smoke, which stem from their moon-
cratered scalps. The glowing seeds of a nightly garden that will
blossom into full moons regardless of the Sun. They know the
night and the seven names of the wind through the tales of their
windblown fathers. Who will father these mothers of light? And
what will become of me?

Children of the night,
only some will star the sky
only believers in death will die
and fathers must feather the wings of women

For the unfeathered masses dangle, ridiculous
carrying crosses to phalanx filled tombs
the future sails silence through blood-rivered wombs
that ripple with riddles of cows and spoons
and births moons and earths, Sun-centered at noon

she buries her eggs in the soil and plants her feet in the sky
soil seeds a circus of carrots and clowns and minstrel shows
our desires

and here I stand
court jestering infinity
fetal-fisted for revolution
but open hands birth humility

Now what is the density of an ego-less planet?

Must my spine be aligned to sprout wings?

I'm slouched into slang steps
and kangol'd with gang reps
but my orbit rainbows Saturn's rings:
mystical elliptical
presto
polaris

karmic flamed future when Saturn's in Aries
and how I'm fish called father
with gills type Dizzy:
blowing liquid lullabies
through the spine of time
to tranquilize a nervous system's defeat

At the feet of forever the children are gathered or rather buried in that mass grave site of the night. They are the seeds of light planted in the sky. But then nights and skies are meaningless to their unearthly eyes.

They are our children:
playing chess on the sunburnt backs of one-eyed turtles
checkmating a lifetime's slow crawl to enlightenment
cashing in their crown and glory for magic and contradiction

the children of fiction
born of semen-filled crosses
thrust in calvary's mound
with memories of mañanas' millennium:
the gravity of the pendulum
the inscription of the grail
the rumors of war and famine
diseases and storms of hail

All hail the new beginning! Behold the winter's end!
Bring on the puppets and dragons!
Let the ceremonies begin

For they have come to shatter time and bring back the dead
Newborn, an army of me:
bearing change on the front lines
and shadows in the field mines
to wilderness the lights of the city

I have seen them:

A tumultuous army of
beggars and bastards
witches and harlots
madmen and idiots
dancers and lunatics
losers and lovers
sinners and singers
students and teachers
poets and priests

orbiting the realms of the ordinary
through the ordinances of those ordained by the beast

These are our children: love-laden life lanterns
casting shadows that shepherd the flocks
crying wolf when the moon's full
as sirens of loves lull
the offspring of Gibraltar's rocks

Who will deny them when thrice crows the cock?

ii

Will it be you Peter?
decked in daymare's denial
masqueraded in matter
over mind
under trial

self is the servant to serpents with wings
three is the beginning of all things
try angles when wrecks tangle your wings
know ye are the sum of your burdens
pile stones and unearth ancient learnings
see self as the ghost of your servings

if you're serving the father
there's no son without mother

parent bodies
discover
water bodies
and drown

wade me in the water
til Atlantis is found

on the sea floor of self
i am starfish and unbound

heard the name of that mound is Stone Mountain
underwater volcanoes
erupt water fountains of youth

lest this carnal equation cancel out wind and truth
swirl me beyond sometimes
drench me waterproof
let eves drop forever
rain sunsets on my roof

as i sit on the front porch of my sanity
deciphering hambones
to van gogh this vanity

"oiled egos canvassed and framed"

to be reborn
unborn
unburied
unnamed

a reflection through a bloodstained glass window
of souls gone yellow round the edges:
carbonated dreams
and blurred daily lives

but let family bring focus
out of swamps blossom lotus

the muddy water blue daughters of infinity
grant us water-bodied bodhisattvas our serenity
as we rise with the tides towards divinity

iii

and she will be raised by wolves
just below the masonry dixon line
where eagles noose the misuse of Osiris's sacred papyrus
in their claws clench
so that the vultures of our memories may feast upon the remedies
of ancient laws
lynched
and flock to the treetops
of the forethoughts we have forgotten

yes, silence will be begotten of the wind

the silver eyes of the darkness are her friends
and they sometimes plant forever in their dens
on the mountainsides of sometimes now and then
in between the rise and set of you and i

may blue visions know the depth of liquid skies

and some ask me if she cries in the night
when it's the substance of her tears
that drench the days with light

shit, you better hope she do

'cause there are women with fur coats and painted faces
they eat Chinese apples that stain their teeth red
and can cackle cosmos out of chaos
at a moment's . . .

notice the children on the train
selling chocolate with their mothers in the background
fundraising their dreams from the dead

and the authors of autumn correspond with catharsis
and change the leaves of my needs orange red

i need fruit and vegetables
for only living things can feed the span of wings

and thus she was born
to charter my flight
into the blues of night

i am the darkness that precedes the light
a pupil of the sea's reflective sight

notebook in hand
i footnote land and write

plot, dot, dot, dot
and dot my "i"s as bright

and cast my lot amongst the children
and the night

afterword

Passivity plays no part in Relation. Every time an individual or community attempts to define its place in it, even if this place is disputed, it helps blow the usual way of thinking off course, driving out the now weary rules of former classicisms, making new "follow-through" to *chaos-monde* possible.

The science of Chaos renounces linearity's potent grip and, in this expanse/extension, conceives of indeterminacy as a fact that can be analyzed and accident as measurable. By rediscovering the abysses of art or the interplay of various aesthetics, scientific knowledge thus develops one of the ways poetics is expressed, reconnecting with poetry's earlier ambition to establish itself as knowledge. . . .

In expanse/extension the forms of *chaos-monde* (the immeasurable intermixing of cultures) are unforeseeable and foretellable. We have not yet begun to calculate their consequences: the passive adoptions, irrevocable rejections, naive beliefs, parallel lives, and the many forms of confrontation or consent, the many syntheses, surpassings, or returns, the many sudden outbursts of invention, born of impacts and breaking what has produced them, which compose the fluid, turbulent, stubborn, and possibly organized matter of our common destiny. . . .

Relation is learning more and more to go beyond judgments into the unexpected dark of art's upsurgings. Its beauty springs from the stable and the unstable, from the deviance of many particular poetics and the clairvoyance of a relational poetics. . . . The highest point of knowledge is always a poetics.

—Édouard Glissant, *The Poetics of Relation*

not<u>es/</u>glossary

Yusef Komunyakaa (Foreword)

Yusef Komunyakaa, originally from Bogalusa, Louisiana,
served in Vietnam as a correspondent and managing editor of the
Southern Cross. Within a five-year period between 1975 and 1980,
he received a B.A. in English and Sociology, an M.A. in Creative
Writing for Poetry at the University of Colorado and Colorado
State University, respectively, and an M.F.A. in Creative Writing
for Poetry at the University of California in Irvine. During the last
twenty years, Komunyakaa has published nine books of poems,
including *Neon Vernacular: New and Selected Poems 1977–1989*
(Wesleyan/New England), winner of the 1994 Pulitzer Prize for
poetry and the Kingsley-Tufts Poetry Award from the Claremont
Graduate School in California. This volume selects from previously
published titles: *Lost in the Bonewheel Factory, Copacetic, I Apolo-
gize for the Eyes in My Head,* and *Dien Cai Dau,* the latter of which
is a virtuosic meditation on the unspoken penalties of war. In *Neon
Vernacular,* Komunyakaa draws upon haunting recollections, his
particular African-American experiences, poignant tributes, and
significant turns of history. However, here, as in much of his poetry,
jazz and the blues imbue the cadences that transport memory
through the serene heart of his own lyrics. *Magic City* (1992)
returns the poet's gaze homeward, to youth, early sexuality, the
endearing lessons from family, and the legacies that sustain a com-
munity. Fully cognizant of sanctimonious borders and increasingly

irreverent of fixed categories, in *Thieves of Paradise* (1998), his most recent volume of poems, Komunyakaa traverses the limits of time and geographies, even more than previously, for the sake of striking out into a mindfulness that an ethical look at society requires. He does this, in part, by designing luminous phrases of varied apertures. Truncated lines focus on momentary images, while those that tarry move into narration requiring the fuller space of a page. Revisiting themes, as he often does, Komunyakaa sings a protracted song, and if injustices appear in a poem, so do the passionate affirmations of what is honorable. On the recording *Love Notes from the Madhouse* (1998), performed live with jazz musician John Tchicai and ensemble, Komunyakaa reads poems from *Neon Vernacular* and *Thieves of Paradise*. With Sascha Feinstein, he coedits *The Jazz Poetry Anthology* and regularly contributes to *Brilliant Corners*, a literary journal edited by Feinstein, also dedicated to the literature of jazz. Recent literary awards include the Union League Civic and Arts Poetry Prize from *Poetry* magazine (1998) and the Hanes Poetry Prize (1997). Komunyakaa is a professor in the Council of Humanities and Creative Writing Program at Princeton University.

Zoë Anglesey (Introduction)

Zoë Anglesey has edited four anthologies—most recently the bilingual collection *Stone on Stone / Piedra Sobre Piedra: Poetry by Women of Diverse Heritages*. She is poetry editor at the *MultiCultural Review*, a contributing editor to *BOMB* magazine, and a regular freelance writer for *Down Beat*, *Jazziz*, and *New York Latino*. She is a former senior editor of the *VLS—The Voice Literary Supplement*. As a poet and translator, Anglesey contributes to literary journals and anthologies. Her most recent translations appear in *Dream with No Name: Contemporary Fiction from Cuba*, edited by Juana Ponce de Leon, and *Boricuas: Influential Puerto Rican Writings*, edited by Roberto Santiago. Currently, Anglesey curates the Literary

Arts Reading Series at Pratt Institute in Brooklyn, New York. Previously, in the mid-1990s, she curated the Meet the Author series at the Brooklyn Moon Café, while in the 1980s, she curated readings, including bilingual presentations of internationally renowned poets, at the Gas Station in Manhattan. Originally from the Pacific Northwest, Anglesey lives in Brooklyn and, as an adjunct professor, teaches writing at the New School University and Medgar Evers College of CUNY.

Édouard Glissant (Afterword)

Originally from the Caribbean island of Martinique, Édouard Glissant, with schoolmate Frantz Fanon, attended classes taught by Aimé Césaire. Rather than following his mentor, Glissant, over a lifetime, has challenged fixed paradigms including that of "negritude." Instead, Glissant relies on history in all its flux—millennia of biological developments, global migrations, human relations, art, language(s), and culture(s)—to propose that relativity also applies to literature. As for translated works available in the United States, there are *Édouard Glissant and Caribbean Discourse: Selected Essays,* translated by Michael J. Dash. *The Ripening,* a novel originally published in France, won the *Prix Renaudot* in 1958. In *The Poetics of Relation,* Glissant presents ideas that poets in *Listen Up!* share. Most relevantly, Glissant writes: "Poetry is not an amusement nor a display of sentiments or beautiful things. It also imparts form to a knowledge that could never be stricken by obsolescence."

Tish Benson

Llegba	Spelled variously, a Yoruba deity (orisha) who is messenger, Trickster, keeper of the gate and crossroads
ital (i'tal)	Jamaican term for nourishing, life-affirming food
Yemenya	Spelled variously, an orisha of the sea, mother of life
Oshun	An orisha of fresh waters, sweetness, money, sensuality
Billie	Billie Holiday, (1915-1959), African-American jazz singer
Bessie	Bessie Smith, (1894-1937), African-American blues/jazz singer

Suheir Hammad

Kaabah	Muslim holy site in Mecca, originally built by Abraham
Zam Zam	Holy well containing divine waters
Safa/Marwah	The two sacred hills that Hagar searched for water in the desert
Bed Stuy/Bushwick	Brooklyn neighborhoods
Sarandils	Adam descended on the island of this name
hajj	Muslim annual pilgrimage to Mecca
Medina	City in Saudi Arabia; the word itself means "city"

Jessica Care Moore

Dun	Nickname for Last Poet Abiodun Oyewole
hero, Heroine	"Hero" is feminine in Greek, the language in which the term originates

Tracie Morris

Badal Roy	Performed with Miles Davis, as in *Black Beauty*. He still tours with jazz groups on the international circuit
Las Brujitas	"Little" or "dear" conjurers who practice pagan or West African rituals
Nommo	Orisha associated with the word
guaguancó	One of three rumba types; a seductive midtempo couple dance
berimbau	A stringed instrument with a calabash for its soundbox
Miles	Miles Davis (1926-1991), monumental jazz trumpeter
Trane	Refers to John Coltrane (1926–1967), an innovative virtuoso on the jazz saxophone and composer
Nat Cole	Nat "King" Cole (1919-1965), known for his innovative jazz trio before becoming a pop singer
Duke	Edward "Duke" Ellington (1899-1974), the great jazz bandleader, composer, and pianist

Willie Perdomo

Bayamón	A Puerto Rican town not far from San Juan in the northeast
Ponce	A Puerto Rican city on the southern coast of the Caribbean Sea
Boricua	Indigenous name for Puerto Rico
y dicen que . . .	And they say that . . .
Poughkeepsie	City in upstate New York
Garrison/Peekskill	Towns in upstate New York
Sing-Sing	Prison in upstate New York
mi gente	My people

Miky	Miguel Piñero, poet, playwright, TV dramatist, and cofounder of the Nuyorican Poets Café
pana	A friend and constant companion
Brixton	A district of London famed for its Jamaican/Caribbean community
Hablas . . .	"You speak . . ." (Spanish, yes, I love you, too)
mami	Cute mommy, girlfriend
papi toito	Means "my cute daddy, my everything"— *toito* is a diminutive of *todo*, or everything
apuñala	Abbreviated and command form of *apuñalar*, which means to stab
mi corazón . . .	(Stab) "my heart" (with your knife of love, my beloved)

Carl Hancock Rux

Césaire	Aimé Césaire (b. 1913) is from Martinique and is one of the founders of the Negritude movement, which influenced the Harlem Renaissance
Garvey's ghost	Refers to "Garvey's Ghost," a composition by great jazz drummer Max Roach
Bali	An island of southern Indonesia east of Java; known as the "jewel of Asia," located between the Java Sea and the Indian Ocean
Denpasar	A province in Bali

works cited

Afrocentrics Spoken Word Newsletter. 85 Sunnyside Street, Hyde Park, Mass. 02136.

Algarín, Miguel. *Love Is Hard Work: Memorias de Loisaida*. New York: Scribner, 1997 (poems).

___ and Lois Griffith, eds. *Action: The Nuyorican Poets Café Theater Festival: Plays, Monologues, and Performance Pieces*. New York: Touchstone / Simon & Schuster, 1997.

___ and Bob Holman, eds. *Aloud: Voices from the Nuyorican Poets Café*. New York: Henry Holt, 1994 (poems).

Anderson, S. E. and Tony Medina, eds. *In Defense of Mumia*. New York: Writers & Readers Publishing, 1996 (poems).

Angelou, Maya. *The Complete Collected Poems of Maya Angelou*. New York: Random House, 1994.

___. *I Know Why the Caged Bird Sings* [1970]. New York: Bantam Books, 1997.

Anglesey, Zoë. *Something More Than Force: Poems for Guatemala 1971–1982*. Easthampton, Mass.: Adastra Press, 1982.

___, ed. *Stone on Stone / Piedra Sobre Piedra: Poetry by Women of Diverse Heritages*: a Bilingual Anthology. Seattle, Wash.: Open Hand Publishing, 1994.

___, ed. *Ixok Amar.Go: Central American Women's Poetry for Peace*. Penobscot, Maine: Granite Press, 1987.

___, ed. *¡Word Up! Hope for Youth Poetry*, Seattle, Wash.: El Centro de la Raza, 1992.

Baldwin, James. *Giovanni's Room* [1956]. New York: Dell, 1973.

Bandele, Asha. *Absence in the Palms of My Hands*. New York: Writers & Readers Publishing, 1996.

Baraka, Amiri. *Funk Lore: New Poems, 1984–1994*. Los Angeles: Sun & Moon Press, 1996.

___. *Transbluency: Poems of Amiri Baraka/LeRoi Jones (1961-1995)*. New York: Marsilio Publishers, 1996.

Blum, Joshua, Bob Holman, and Mark Pellington, comps. *The United States of Poetry*. New York: Abrams, 1996.

Bonnette, Pierre. *The Jelly Bean Tree*. New York: Moore Black Press, forthcoming.

Boyle, T. Coraghessan, et al., eds. *It's Only Rock and Roll: An Anthology of Rock and Roll*. Boston: David R. Godine, 1998.

Cabico, Regie and Todd Swift, eds. *Poetry Nation: A North American Anthology of Fusion Poetry*. New York: Vehicule Press, 1998.

Césaire, Aimé. *Notebook of Return to My Native Land*. England: Bloodaxe Books, 1995 (poems).

Chametzky, Jules, ed. *Black Writers Redefine the Struggle: A Tribute to James Baldwin*. Amherst, Mass.: University of Massachusetts Press, 1989.

Cheever, John. *The World of Apples*. New York: Alfred A. Knopf, 1973.

Coleridge, Samuel Taylor. *Selected Poetry*. Edited by H. J. Jackson. New York: Oxford University Press, 1997.

Duffy, Dan, ed. *Not a War: American Vietnamese Fiction, Poetry, and Essays*. New Haven: Yale University Council of Southeast Asia Studies. Yale Center for International and Area Studies, 1987.

El Saadawi, Nawal. *The Nawal El Saadawi Reader*. London: Zed Books, 1997.

Feinstein, Sascha and Yusef Komunyakaa, eds. *The Jazz Poetry Anthology*. Bloomington: Indiana University Press, 1991.

___. *The Second Set*. Volume 2. Bloomington: Indiana University Press, 1996.

Fernando, S. H., Jr. *The New Beats: Exploring the Music, Culture, and Attitudes of Hip-Hop*. New York: Doubleday, 1994.

Gaines, Reg E. *Original Buckwheat* (poems). Hoboken, N.J.: Long Shot Productions, 1998.

García Márquez, Gabriel. *Leaf Storm and Other Stories*. Translated by Gregory Rebassa [1972]. New York: HarperCollins, 1979.

___. *One Hundred Years of Solitude*. Translated by Gregory Rebassa [1970]. New York: HarperCollins, 1991.

Genet, Jean. *The Blacks: A Clown Show*. Translated by Bernard Frechtman. New York: Grove Press, 1976.

Gilbert, Derrick I. and Tony Medina, eds. *Catch the Fire!!!: A Cross-Generational Anthology of Contemporary African-American Poetry*. New York: Riverhead Books/Putnam, 1998.

Giles, Fiona, ed. *Dick for a Day: What Would You Do If You Had One?* New York: Villard Books/ Random House, 1997 (stories).

Gilyard, Keith, ed. *Spirit & Flame: An Anthology of Contemporary African American Poetry*. Syracuse, N.Y.: Syracuse University Press, 1997.

Giovanni, Nikki. *Ego-Tripping and Other Poems for Young People*. 2nd rev. ed. Chicago: Lawrence Hill Books, 1993.

___. *The Selected Poems of Nikki Giovanni*. New York: William Morrow, 1996.

Glissant, Édouard. *Caribbean Discourse: Selected Essays*. Translated by J. Michael Dash. Charlottesville: University Press of Virginia, 1989.

___. *Faulkner, Mississippi*. Translated by Barbara Lewis and Thomas C. Spear. New York: Farrar Straus & Giroux, 1999.

___. *Poetics of Relation*. Translated by Betsy Wing. Ann Arbor: The University of Michigan Press, 1997.

Guillory, Monique and Richard C. Greene, eds. *Soul: Black Power, Politics, and Pleasure*. New York: New York University Press, 1998.

Hammad, Suheir. *Born Palestinian, Born Black*. New York: Published for Harlem River Press by Writers & Readers Publishing, 1996 (poems).

___. *Drops of This Story*. New York: Published for Harlem River Press by Writers & Readers Publishing, 1996 (memoir).

Hughes, Danne, ed. *Poetry on Stage: At the Red Barn Theatre*. Key West: Poho Press, 1995.

Hughes, Langston. *The Collected Poems of Langston Hughes*. Edited by Arnold Rampersad. New York: Vintage Classics/Random House, 1995.

___.*Selected Poems of Langston Hughes*. New York: Vintage Classics/Random House, 1990.

Joans, Ted. *Teducation: Known and Unknown Selected Poems of Ted Joans*. Minneapolis, Minn.: Coffee House Press, 1999.

Jones, Hettie. *How I Became Hettie Jones*. New York: Grove/Atlantic, 1997.

Jordan, June. *Things That I Do in the Dark: Selected Poetry*. New York: Random House, 1977.

Kinnell, Galway. *The Avenue Bearing the Initial of Christ into the New World, Poems 1946–64*. Boston: Houghton Mifflin, 1974.

Komunyakaa, Yusef. *Dien Cai Dau*. Hanover, N.H.: Wesleyan University Press/University Press of New England, 1988.

___. *Magic City*. Hanover, N.H.: Wesleyan University Press/University Press of New England, 1992.

___. *Neon Vernacular: New and Selected Poems*. Hanover, N.H.: Wesleyan University Press/University Press of New England, 1993.

___. *Thieves of Paradise*. Hanover, N.H.: Wesleyan University Press/University Press of New England, 1998 (poems).

LeFanu, Sarah, ed. *Sex, Drugs, Rock 'n' Roll: Stories to the End of the Century*. London: Serpents Tail, 1987; Boston: David R. Godine, 1998.

Lorde, Audre. *The Collected Poems of Audre Lorde*. New York: W. W. Norton, 1997.

Madhubuti, Haki R. *Groundwork: New and Selected Poems of Don L. Lee/Haki R. Madhubuti,1966–1996*. Chicago: Third World Press, 1996.

____. *Heart Love: Wedding and Love Poems*. Chicago: Third World Press, 1998.

McDonnell, Evelyn and Ann Powers, eds. *Rock She Wrote: Women Write about Rock, Pop, and Rap*. New York: Delta/Dell, 1995.

McKay, Claude. *Home to Harlem* [1928]. Boston: Northeastern University Press, 1987.

____. *Harlem Glory: A Fragment of American Life*. Reprint. New York: Charles H. Kerr Publishing, 1991.

Medina, Tony. *Sermons from the Smell of a Carcass Condemned to Begging*. Hoboken, N.J.: Long Shot Productions, 1998 (poems).

Miller, E. Ethelbert. *Where Are the Love Poems for Dictators?* [1986]. Seattle, Wash.: Open Hand Publishers, 1994 (poems).

____. *Whispers, Secrets and Promises*. Baltimore: Black Classic Press, 1998 (poems).

____. ed. *Beyond the Frontier*. Baltimore: Black Classic Press, 1999 (anthology of poetry).

Moore, Jessica Care. *The Words Don't Fit in My Mouth*. New York: Moore Black Press, 1997 (poems).

Morris, Tracie. *Chap-T-her Won*. Brooklyn: TM Ink, 1993.

____. *Intermission*. New York: Soft Skull Press, 1998.

Muller, Lauren and the Blueprint Collective. *June Jordan's Poetry for the People: A Revolutionary Blueprint*. New York: Routledge, 1995.

Oyewole, Abiodun and Umar Bin Hassan with Kim Green. *The Last Poets on a Mission: Selected Poems and a History of the Last Poets* (with Kim Green, Foreword by Amiri Baraka). New York: Henry Holt, 1996.

Perdomo, Willie. *Where a Nickel Costs a Dime*. New York: W. W. Norton, 1996 (poems).

Ponce de Leon, Juana, ed. *Dream with No Name: Contemporary Fiction from Cuba*. New York: Seven Stories Press, 1998.

Powell, Kevin, and Ras Baraka, eds. *In the Tradition: An Anthology of Young Black Writers*. New York: Published for Harlem River Press by Writers & Readers Publishing, 1992.

Reeves, Gareth. *T. S. Eliot's The Waste Land: Critical Studies of Key Texts*. New York: Harvester Wheatsheaf, 1994.

Robeson, Paul. *Here I Stand* [1958]. Boston: Beacon Press, 1988.

Ruff, Shawn Stewart, ed. *Go the Way Your Blood Beats: An Anthology of Lesbian and Gay Fiction by African-American Writers*. New York: Henry Holt, 1996.

Rux, Carl Hancock. *Pagan Operetta*. New York: Fly by Night Press, 1998 (poems).

Salaam, Kalamu Ya and Kwame Alexander, eds. *360 Degrees: A Revolution of Black Poets*. New Orleans: BlackWords, 1998.

Sanchez, Sonia. *Does Your House Have Lions?* Boston: Beacon Press, 1997.

___. *Like the Singing Coming Off the Drums: Love Poems*. Boston: Beacon Press, 1998.

Santiago, Roberto, ed. *Boricuas: Influential Puerto Rican Writings— an Anthology*. New York: One World/Ballantine Books, 1995.

Senghor, Léopold Sédar. *The Collected Poetry*. Translated by Melvin Dixon. Charlottesville: University Press of Virginia, 1991.

Shange, Ntozake. *for colored girls who have considered suicide when the rainbow is enuf* [1975]. New York: Simon & Schuster, 1997.

Simmons, Sharrif. *Fubraction*. New York: Moore Black Press, 1998 (poems).

Stratton, Richard and Kim Wozencraft, eds. *Slam*. New York: Grove/Atlantic Press, 1998.

Thomas, Piri. *Down These Mean Streets* [1967;1974]. New York: Vintage/Random House, 1997.

Trachtenberg, Jordan and Amy Trachtenberg, eds. *Verses That Hurt: Pleasure and Pain from the Poemfone Poets*. New York: St. Martin's Press, 1997.

Troupe, Quincy. *Avalanche*. Minneapolis, Minn: Coffee House Press, 1996 (poems).

___. *Weather Reports: New and Selected Poems*. New York: Writers & Readers Publishing, 1991.

Turk, Tara. *Sugar Doe: A Novel.* New York: Moore Black Press, 1998.

Waldman, Anne, ed. *Out of This World: An Anthology of the St. Mark's Poetry Project 1966–1991.* New York: Crown, 1991.

Walker, Alice. *Anything We Love Can Be Saved.* New York: Ballantine Books/Random House, 1997, 1998.

___. *Revolutionary Petunias & Other Poems* [1973]. Boston: Harcourt Brace, 1984.

Weaver, Michael S. *My Father's Geography.* Pitt Poetry Series. Pittsburgh: University of Pittsburgh Press, 1992.

Wilentz, Elias, ed. *The Beat Scene.* New York: Corinth Books, 1960.

Williams, Saul Stacey. *Children of the Night.* Staple Crop Press, 1996.

___. *The Seventh Octave: The Early Writings of Saul Williams.* New York: Moore Black Press, 1998.

___. Untitled. New York: Pocket Books/Simon & Schuster, forthcoming, poems.

Wright, Richard. *Native Son* [1940]. New York: HarperCollins, 1993.

___. *Black Boy* [1945]. New York: HarperCollins, 1998.

discography

Ailey, Alvin. *A Musical Retrospective on Forty Years of Dance.* V2 Records, 1998.

Allen, Tyren. *MISC: Experiences.* Fifth Child, 1998.

Baraka, Ras. *Shorty for Mayor.* Jamaican Niché Records, 1998.

Black Whole Styles. Ninja 2, 1998. English label, with Saul Williams.

Eargasms. Ozone/Mercury Records, 1997. Compilation with Last Poets, Saul Williams, Jessica Care Moore, Carl Hancock Rux, et al.

Emily XYZ. *Take What You Can Live.* Alek, 1998. With Tracie Morris.

Flippin the Script: Rap Meets Poetry. Mouth Almighty Records/Mercury Records, 1996. Compilation with Tish Benson, Willie Perdomo, et al.

Gaines, Reg E. *Deaf Music.* Hush Records, 1997. With Saul Williams.

___. *Please Don't Take My Air Jordans.* Mercury Records, 1994.

___. *Sweeper Don't Clean My Streets.* Mercury Records, 1995. With Rux.

Harris, Kevin Bruce. *Folk Songs/Folk Tales.* Enja Records, 1994. With Tracie Morris's "Skins."

Hart, Antonio. *Here I Stand.* Impulse, 1997. Grammy-nominated track with Jessica Care Moore.

Haynes, Graham. *Tones for the 21st Century.* Verve/Forecast, 1998. With Tracie Morris's "Out of Phase/Trans-gression."

Irvine, Weldon. *Spoken Melodies.* Nodlew Music, 1997. With Saul Williams.

Komunyakaa, Yusef and Tchicai. *Love Notes from the Madhouse,* 8th Harmonic Breakdown, 1998. Jazz/spoken word.

Lyricist's Lounge. Open Mic. Rawkus Records, 1998. Compilation featuring Saul Williams, Q-tip, De La Soul, KRS-1, et al.

The Mango Room. Hardboiled Entertainment, 1999. Compilation with Tish Benson, T'Kalla, Tyren Allen, et al.

Mingus, Charles. *The Clown.* Atlantic Records, 1957. Includes "Haitian Fight Song."

___. *Let My Children Hear Music.* Columbia Records / CBS.

___. *Mingus, Mingus, Mingus.* Impulse, 1963. Includes "II B.S"–rendition of "Haitian Fight Song."

Morrison, Jim. *The Ultimate Collected Spoken . . . .* Cleopatra, 1998. Boxed set.

Nuyorican Symphony. Knitting Factory Works, 1993. With Tracie Morris.

Parker, Leon. *Awakening.* Columbia/SONY, 1998. With Tracie Morris on "All My Life."

Reid, Vernon and Living Colour. *Vivid.* Epic Records, 1991. Tracie Morris cowrote "Open Letter to a Landlord."

Rux, Carl Hancock. *Rux Revue.* SONY 550 MUSIC, 1999.

Sharp, Elliot. *SOTU.* P.S. 1 Contemporary Art Center (http://www.ps1.org), 1997. With Tracie Morris on track 27.

___. *State of the Union*. Atavistic Records, 1994. With Tracie Morris's "Prelude to a Kiss."

___. *Time Bomb*. P. S. 1 Contemporary Art Center (http://www.ps1.org), 1997. With Tracie Morris.

SLAM. Immortal/Epic, 1998. Sound track with Saul Williams, Sonja Sohn, KRS-1.

SoulCoughing. *El Oso*. Warner Bros., 1998.

Williams, Saul Stacey. *She*. American Recordings/SONY, forthcoming.

film and video

Half a Lifetime: A Documentary. Features Suheir Hammad, Pariah Productions/ Refugee Camp Productions (Butter Phoenix@yahoo.com), forthcoming.

Slam. 1998. Directed by Marc Levin. A feature-length film. Grand Jury Prize, 1998 Sundance Film Festival, Caméra d'Or Prix du Public at the 1998 Cannes Film Festival.

Slam Nation: A Documentary. 1998. Directed by Paul Devlin.

Spicy City. HBO, 1997. Cowritten by Willie Perdomo.

Underground Voices: A Documentary. 1997. Directed by Reg E. Gaines.

The United States of Poetry. 1996. Washington Square Films. Directed by Mark Pellington.

Words in Your Face. 1990. Washington Square Films. Directed by Mark Pellington.